MYSTERY
Experiencing the Mystery of God

Paul E. Stroble

Abingdon Press
Nashville

Mystery: Experiencing the Mystery of God
20/30: Bible Study for Young Adults

by Paul E. Stroble

Copyright © 2002 by Abingdon Press

ISBN 0-687-09770-3

This book is printed on acid-free paper.

MANUFACTURED IN THE UNITED STATES OF AMERICA.

02 03 04 05 06 07 08 09 10 11—10 9 8 7 6 5 4 3 2 1

CONTENTS

Meet the Writer 4

Welcome to *20/30* 5

How to Use This Resource 7

Organizing a Group 9

Preparing to Lead 11

Choosing Teaching Options 13

Using Break-Out Groups 15

Mystery: Experiencing the Mystery of God 17

Session 1:
Unpacking the Mystery in *Mystery* 19

Session 2:
God's Mysterious Presence 27

Session 3:
The Holy Spirit 35

Session 4:
Spiritual Formation 43

Session 5:
What Are Spiritual Disciplines? 51

Session 6:
How Am I Supposed to Worship? 59

Session 7:
Put It All Together. 67

Case Studies 75

Service Learning Options 78

MEET THE WRITER

PAUL E. STROBLE, an ordained elder of The United Methodist Church, teaches in the history and honors departments at the University of Akron. He is married to Beth, who is dean of the School of Education at the University of Akron. They are parents of twelve-year-old Emily. A native of Vandalia, Illinois, Paul studied at Greenville College, Yale Divinity School, and the University of Virginia. He has taught a wide range of courses in philosophy, religious studies, history, New Testament, and world religion. He has also served in a variety of parish roles as pastor, minister of programs, and volunteer leader.

Paul is the author of seven other books including the Abingdon study book *Paul and the Galatians*; a novel, *Adams Street Antiques*; and a monograph, *High on the Okaw's Western Bank: Vandalia, Illinois, 1819-1839*. He writes for *FaithLink* and has written numerous papers and articles for religious publications, articles on various historical subjects, essays for regional magazines, and poetry.

Paul enjoys drawing and photography, shopping in antique stores, doing almost anything with Beth and Emily, and looking under furniture for cats Odd Ball and Domino.

WELCOME TO 20/30: BIBLE STUDY FOR YOUNG ADULTS

The *20/30* Bible study series is offered for post-modern adults who want to help structure their own discoveries—in life, in relationships, in faith. In each of the volumes of this series, you will have the opportunity to use your personal experiences in life and faith to examine the biblical texts in new ways. Each session offers biblical themes and images that have the power to shape contemporary human life.

The Power of Images

An image has evocative power. You can see, hear, smell, taste, and touch the image in your imagination. It also has the power to evoke memory and to inform ideas and feelings. Placing Christmas ornaments on a tree evokes memories of past Christmas celebrations or of circumstances surrounding the acquisition of the ornament. As an adult you may remember making the ornament as a gift for your mother, father, or another important person in your life. You may experience once again all the feelings you had when you gave this gift.

An image also informs and gives shape to themes and ideas like hope, faith, love, and compassion. The image of the ornament gives a particular shape to love because each Christmas someone carefully places it on the tree. Love becomes specific and easy to identify.

Biblical Images

The Bible offers an array of powerful and evocative images through stories, parables, poems, proverbs, and sermons. Jesus used a variety of familiar images: a woman seeking a lost coin, a merchant finding a pearl, seeds and plants, and cups that are clean on the outside but dirty on the inside. Such images transcend time and place and speak to people today. A story about a Samaritan who helped a wounded person says far more than the simple assertion that loving a neighbor means *being* a neighbor. Each of the volumes in this series connects familiar, contemporary experiences with scriptural content through a shared knowledge of theme and image.

Mystery: Experiencing the Mystery of God
Grace: Being Loved, Loving God
Balance: Living With Life's Demands
Abundance: Living Responsibly With God's Gifts
Love: Opening Your Heart to God and Others
Faith: Living a Spirited Life
Covenant: Making Commitments That Count
Exodus: Leaving Behind, Moving On
Community: Living Faithfully With Others

Experience, Faith, Growth, and Action

Each volume in this series is designed to help you explore ways in which your experience links with your faith and how deepening your faith expands your life experiences. As a prompt for reflection, each volume has several real-life case studies. Ways to be involved in specific service opportunities are listed on pages 78-80. Activities in each session suggest ways to engage you or a group with the themes and images in the Bible.

A core Christian belief affirms that God's graceful presence and activity moves through all creation. This series is designed to support your encounters with God in a community of faith through Scripture, reflection, and dialogue. One goal of such encounters is to enhance your individual and shared commitment to serve others in the hope that they too might experience God's graceful presence.

HOW TO USE THIS RESOURCE

Each session of this resource includes similar components or elements:
- a statement of the issue or question to be explored
- several "voices" of persons who are currently dealing with that issue
- exploration of biblical passages relating to the question raised
- "Bible 101" boxes that provide insight about the study of the Bible
- questions for reflection and discussion
- suggested individual and group activities designed to bring the session to life
- optional case studies (found in the back of the book)
- various service learning activities related to the session (found in the back of the book)

Choices, Choices, Choices

Collectively, these components mean one thing: *choice*. You have choices to make concerning how to use each session of this resource. Want just the nitty-gritty Bible reading, reflection, and study for personal or group use? Then focus your attention on just those components during your study time.

Like starting with real-life stories about issues then moving into how the Bible might be relevant? Start with the "voices" and move on from there. Use the "voices" to encourage group members to speak about their own experiences.

Prefer highly charged discussion encounters where many different viewpoints can be heard? Start the session with the biblical passages, followed by the questions and group activities. Be sure to compare the ideas found in the "Biblical Studies 101" boxes with your current ideas for more discussion. Want the major challenge of applying biblical principles to a difficult problem? After reading the biblical material, read one of the case studies, using the guidelines provided on page 14, or get involved with one of the service learning options described on pages 78-80.

Great Versatility

This resource has been designed for many different uses. Some persons will use this resource for personal study and reflection. Others will want to explore the work with a small group of friends. And still others will see this book as a different type of Sunday school resource.

Spend some time thinking about your own questions, study habits, and learning styles or those of your small group. Then use the guidelines mentioned above to fashion each session into a unique Bible study session to meet those requirements.

Highly Participatory

As you will see, the Scriptures, "voices," commentary, and experiences of group members will provide an opportunity for an active, engaging time together. The greatest challenge for a group leader might be "crowd control" —being sure everyone has the chance to put his or her ideas into the mix!

The Scriptures will help you and those who study with you make connections between real-life issues and the Bible. This resource values and encourages personal participation as a means to understand fully and appreciate the intersection of personal belief with God's ongoing work in each and every life.

ORGANIZING A GROUP

Learning with a small group of persons offers certain advantages over studying by yourself. First, you will hopefully encounter different opinions and ideas, making the experience of Bible study a richer and more challenging event. Second, any leadership responsibilities can be shared among group members. Third, different persons will bring different talents. Some will be deep thinkers while other group members will be creative giants. Some persons will be newcomers to the Bible; their questions and comments will help others clarify their deeply held assumptions.

So how does one go about forming a small group? Follow the steps below and see how easy this task can be.

- **Read through the resource carefully.** Think about the ideas presented, the questions raised, and the exercises suggested. If the sessions of this work excite you, it will be easier for you to spread your enthusiasm to others.

- **Spend some time thinking about church members, friends, and coworkers who might find the sessions of this resource interesting**. On a sheet of paper, list two characteristics or talents you see in each person that would make him or her an attractive Bible study group member. Some talents might include "deep thinker," "creative wizard," or "committed Christian." Remember: The best small group has members who differ in learning styles, talents, ideas, and convictions, but who respect the dignity and integrity of the other members.

- **Make a list of potential group members that doubles your target number.** Most functional small groups have seven to fifteen members. If you would like a small group of seven to fifteen members, be prepared to invite fourteen to twenty persons.

- **Once your list of potential candidates is complete, decide on a tentative location and time.** Of course, the details can be negotiated with those persons who accept the invitation, but you need to sound definitive and clear to perspective group members. "We will initially set Wednesday night from 7 to 9 P.M. at my house for our meeting time" will sound more attractive than "Well, I don't know either when or where we would be meeting, but I hope you will consider joining us."

- **Make initial contact with prospective group members short, sweet, and to the point.** Say something like, "We are putting together a Bible study using a different kind of resource. When would be a good time to show you the resource and talk about the study?" Establishing a special time to make the invitation takes the pressure off the prospective group member to make a quick decision.

- **Show up at the decided time and place.** Talk with each prospective member individually. Bring a copy of the resource with you. Show each person what excites you about the study and mention the two unique characteristics or talents you feel he or she would offer the group. Tell each person the initial meeting time and location and how many weeks the small group will meet. Also mention that the need for a new time or location could be discussed during the first group meeting. Ask for a commitment to come to the first session. Thank individuals for their time.

- **Give a quick phone call or e-mail to thank all persons for their consideration and interest.** Remind persons of the time and location of the first meeting.

- **Be organized.** Use the first group meeting to get acquainted. Briefly describe the seven sessions. Have a book for each group member, and discuss sharing responsibilities for leadership.

PREPARING TO LEAD

So the responsibility to lead the group has fallen upon you? Don't sweat it. Follow these simple suggestions and not only will you prepare to lead, you will also find that your mind and heart are open to encounter the Christ who is with you.

■ **Pray.** Find a quiet place. Have your Bible, the *20/30* book, paper, and pen handy. Ask for God's guidance and inspiration as you prepare for the session.

■ **Read.** Look up all the Bible passages. Take careful notes about the ideas, statements, questions, and activities in the session. Jot down ideas and insights that occur to you as you read.

■ **Think about group members.** Which ones like to think about ideas, concepts, or problems? Which ones need to "feel into" an idea by storytelling, worship, prayer, or group activities? Which ones are the "actors" who prefer a hands-on or participatory approach? Which ones might help you lead the session? Pray for each of the persons.

■ **Think about the learning area and supplies.** What might you do with the place where you meet in order to enhance the experiences and activities of the session? Make a list of things like poster board, pens or pencils, paper, markers, large white paper, supplies for more creative activities, Bibles, music, hymnals, or any other supplies you might need for the activities in the session.

■ **Think about special arrangements.** You may need to make special arrangements: inviting a guest speaker, planning an activity that occurs outside the regular time and place, or acquiring audio-visual equipment, for example.

■ **Pray.** After you have thought through all the steps listed above, thank God for insights and inspiration about leading the group.

Using the Activity Icons

20/30 volumes include activity boxes marked with icons or images that indicate the kind of activity described in the box. The icons are intended to help you make decisions about which activities will best meet the needs of your group.

Start A get-acquainted activity that introduces the focus of the session.

 Discuss Activities designed to stimulate large group discussion.

 Small Group Activities designed to stimulate discussion and reflection in groups of two or three persons. See the section "Using Break-Out Groups" on pages 15-16.

 Bible A Bible study activity that lists specific Scriptures. Participants will use the Bible.

 Look Closer An activity designed to promote deeper, reflective awareness for an individual or for a group. The activity may call for use of resources like Bible dictionaries or commentaries.

 Create An activity designed for using a variety of creative art forms: drawing, sculpting, creating a mobile or a collage, or writing a poem or story.

 Case Study An activity designed to explore and discuss a unique case study related to the session content or one of the case studies included in the back of the book.

 Serve An activity that invites the group to discuss and engage in service to others. May relate directly to session content or to one of the service options in the back of the book.

 Music An activity that uses music. May invite listening to a CD or singing a hymn, for example.

 Close A closing activity that invites worship, celebration, or commitment to some specific action as a result of experiencing the session.

CHOOSING TEACHING OPTIONS

This young adult series was designed, written, and produced out of an understanding of the attributes, concerns, joys, and faith issues of young adults. With great care and integrity, this image-based print resource was developed to connect biblical events and relationships with contemporary, real-life situations of young adults. Its pages will promote Christian relationships and community, support new biblical learning, encourage spiritual development, and empower faithful decision making and action.

This study is well suited to young adults and may be used confidently and effectively. But with the great diversity within the young adult population, not every line of this study will be written "just for you." To be most relevant, some portions of the study material need to be tailored to fit your particular group. Adjustments for a good fit involve making choices from options offered by the resource. This customizing may be done easily by a designated leader who is familiar with the layout of the resource and the young adults who are using it.

What to Expect

In this study Scripture and real-life images mesh together to provoke a personal response. Young adults will find themselves thinking, feeling, imagining, questioning, making decisions, professing faith, building connections, inviting discipleship, taking action, and making a difference. Scripture is at the core of each session. Scenarios weave in the dimensions of real life. Narrative and text boxes frame plenty of teaching options to offer young adults.

Each session is part of a cohesive volume, but it is also designed to stand alone. One session is not dependent on knowledge or experience accumulated from other sessions. A group leader can freely choose from the teaching options in an individual session without wondering how it might affect the other sessions.

A Good Fit

For a better fit, alter the session based on what is known about the young adult participants. Young adults are a diverse constituency with varied experiences, interests, needs, and values. There is really no single defining characteristic that links young adults. Specific information about the age, employment status, household, personal relationships, and lifestyle among participants will equip a leader to make choices that ensure a good fit.

■ **Customize.** Read through the session. Notice how scenarios and teaching options move from integrating Scripture and real-life dimensions to inviting a response.

■ **Look at the case studies.** How real is the presentation of real life? Say that the main character is a professional white male, married, in his early twenties, and caught in a workplace dilemma that entangles his immediate superior and a subordinate from his division. Perhaps your group members are mostly college students and recent graduates, unmarried, and still on the way to being "settled." There are many differences between the man in the scenario and these group members.

As a leader, you could choose to eliminate the case study, substitute it with another scenario (there are several more choices on pages 75-77), claim the validity of the dilemma and shift the spotlight from the main character to the subordinate, or modify the description of the main character. Break-out groups based on age or employment experience might also be used to accommodate the differences and offer a better fit.

■ **Look at the teaching options.** How are the activities propelling participants toward a personal response? Perhaps the Scripture study requires more meditative quiet than is possible and a more academic, verbal, or artistic approach would offer a better fit. Maybe more direct decisions or actions would fit better than passive or logical means. Try to keep a balance, though, that allows participants to "get out of their head" to reflect and also to move toward action.

Conceivably, there could be too much in any one session. As a leader, you can pick and choose among teaching options, substitute case studies, take two meetings to do one session, and adapt any process to make a better fit. The tailoring process can be evaluated as adjustments are made. Judge the fit every time you meet. Ask questions that gauge relevance, and assess how the resource has stretched minds, encouraged discipleship, and changed lives.

USING BREAK-OUT GROUPS

20/30 break-out groups are small groups that encourage the personal sharing of lives and the gospel. The word *break-out* is a sweeping term that includes a variety of small group settings. A break-out group may resemble a Bible study group, an interest group, a sharing group, or other types of Christian fellowship groups.

Break-out groups offer young adults a chance to belong and personally relate to one another. Members are known, nurtured, and heard by others. Young adults may agree and disagree while maximizing the exchange of ideas, information, or options. They might explore, confront, and resolve personal issues and feelings with empathy and support. Participants can challenge and hold one another accountable to a personalized faith and stretch its links to real life and service.

Forming Break-Out Groups

As you look through this book, you will see an icon that says "small group." The nature of these small break-out groups will depend on the context and design of the specific session. On occasion the total group of participants will be divided for a particular activity. Break-out groups will differ from one session to the next. Variations may involve the size of the group, how group members are divided, or the task of the group. Break-out groups may also be used to accommodate differences and help tailor the session plan for a better fit. In some sessions, specific group assembly instructions will be provided. For other sessions, decisions regarding the size or division of small groups will be made by the designated leader. Break-out groups may be in the form of pairs or trios, family-sized groups of three to six members, or groups of up to ten members.

They may be arranged simply by grouping persons seated next to one another or in more intentional ways by common interests, characteristics, or life experiences. Consider creating break-out groups according to age; gender; type of household, living arrangements, or love relationships; vocation, occupation, career, or employment status; common or built-in connections; lifestyle; values or perspective; or personal interests or traits.

Membership

The membership of break-out groups will vary from session to session, or even within specific sessions. Young adults need to work at knowing and being known, so that there can be a balance between break-out groups that are more similar and those that reflect greater diversity. There may be times when more honest communication, trust, or accountability may be desired, and group leaders will need to be free to self-select members for small groups.

It is important for *20/30* break-out groups to practice acceptance and to value the worth of others. The potential for small groups to encourage personal sharing and significant relationships is enhanced when members agree to exercise active listening skills, keep confidences, expect authenticity, foster trust, and develop ways of loving one another. All group members contribute to the development and function of break-out groups. Designated leaders especially need to model manners of hospitality and help ensure that each group member is respected.

Invitational Listening

Consider establishing an "invitational listening" routine that validates the perspective and affirms the voice of each group member. After a question or statement is posed, pause and allow time to think—not all persons think on their feet or talk out loud to think. Then, initiate conversation by inviting one group member, by name, to talk. This person may either choose to talk or to "pass." Either way, this person is honored and is offered an opportunity to speak and to be heard. This person carries on the ritual by inviting another group member, by name, to speak. The process continues until all have been invited, by name, to talk. As each one invites another, the responsibility of acceptance and hospitality in the break-out groups is shared among all its members.

Study group members break-out to belong, to share the gospel, to care, and to watch over one another in Christian love. "So deeply do we care for you that we are determined to share with you not only the gospel of God but also our own selves, because you have become very dear to us" (1 Thessalonians 2:8).

MYSTERY:
EXPERIENCING
THE MYSTERY OF GOD

Kasie: I'd say I'm spiritual but not at all religious. Church just seems like a big dress-up place where they hook people through fear of the afterlife. I enjoy my life too much for that. I can't stand the hypocrisy.

Anthony: Some churches prey on people's fear of hell. But I attend a large church where Jesus is really celebrated. You don't have to get all dressed up. You come away with a warm, positive feeling.

Kwame: I just feel that God is everywhere. You want to go to church and talk to him? Then talk. You want to sit in your room or go to a ballgame and talk to God? Talk. God will listen to you wherever you are.

Anisa: I grew up in one denomination, but when I left home I started attending another church. I really like the minister's sermons. They speak to me where I am. In our Sunday school class we've started a program to help the local women's shelter.

Michael: My aunt wants me to go to church with her. They talk a lot about the "Holy Ghost." They like to speak in "tongues." I have no idea what that's all about!

Julie: I don't either. Personally, I'm a very scientific person. I'm more comfortable with what can be explained than with ideas you can't prove.

When you say the word *mystery*, you probably think of different things. You may think of stories by popular authors such as P. D. James, Agatha Christie, Elmore Leonard, Dorothy Sayers, Rex Stout, and many others. In their stories, unexpected and unexplained things, usually crimes, happen. In the end everyone knows the truth, and the mystery is solved.

Christianity is a "whodunit" kind of story in the sense that God's mysteries of love, grace, and salvation are revealed through Jesus Christ (Colossians 2:2-3; 1 Timothy 3:16). Jesus died and rose from the dead. Through his resurrection, we have the gift of God's Spirit who imparts life and blessing to us. God gives us some of the answers to our deepest questions so that when we are lost and uncertain, we know truth and have hope (Colossians 3:1-4).

"Mystery" can also refer to things that defy explanation. Some people believe in UFOs. Some people believe in ghosts. In these cases evidence may be personal experience. You are not likely to believe someone who claims to have seen a UFO unless you have had a similar experience.

Christianity also has something of that mysterious, personal quality. Some people have had disillusioning encounters with organized religion. They

---

17

react skeptically when someone claims to have had a certain religious experience—a physical healing, for instance, or speaking in tongues. Some people are very open to spirituality, but they are not sure the church is the place to find it. Others find very meaningful spiritual experiences in church services or small church groups, but they find it hard to communicate their experience to someone of a different mindset.

In other words, different people have different kinds of experiences, both good and bad. Many of us do not realize that God's Holy Spirit can speak to us in many different kinds of ways. Unfortunately, some Christians absolutize their own spiritual experiences. Because God speaks to them in a certain way, through particular styles of music, through certain kinds of worship, or through other specific kinds of religious actions, they think that God should speak to everyone that same way.

Part of what we will do in *Mystery: Experiencing the Mystery of God* is to explore different ways God speaks to us. The realization that there are different styles of spirituality can be rewarding to you if Christianity has been presented to you in a one-sided way. Such a realization can also be discouraging if you are comfortable with one or two ways of being religious.

God's Holy Spirit *comes to us as we are.* The Spirit does not come merely as a kind of inward, personal validation. The Spirit calls us to a life of continual discovery, service, and faith. God reveals God's plans for the world so we can be partners in the redemption of the world through Christ because we are God's children (Ephesians 1:5-10).

The twentieth-century theologian Dietrich Bonhoeffer wrote about "the God of the gaps." People once attributed to God the things they did not understand. As scientific knowledge advanced, people did not need God as an explanation for as many gaps in their knowledge. Bonhoeffer believed that God does not need to serve as a supplement to science. In our contemporary society, we are tempted to apply scientific measurement to religious things. Churches have to have a certain number of members to be satisfactory. We have to pray for a certain number of minutes each day. We have to have a particular kind of experience to be truly spiritual.

Bonhoeffer preferred not to relate to God in that way. Rather, God is Lord of the whole of life; no part of life is outside God's love and care. We still do not understand everything about science or about ourselves and our place in the world. In these lessons we will consider some of the ways that God, through the Holy Spirit, mysteriously fills our lives.

UNPACKING THE MYSTERY IN MYSTERY

This session examines mystery and types of spirituality.

THE GOD OF FAITH

Julie: A few years ago I took a philosophy course in college. The professor said that we couldn't know God the same way we can know everyday things. God's not available for observation and scientific scrutiny. That made sense to me. But one guy in the back row got very emotional. He said we could know God through faith, through miracles, through prayer, and through the Bible. The professor was nice; she didn't make fun of what he said. But she explained that knowing God is a different sort of knowledge. She said that we know God through faith, but that's a different kind of certainty than scientific observation. The guy seemed really threatened though. To him, prayer, miracles, and the Bible were absolutely reliable ways to know God. He didn't see the professor's point.

Introduce yourselves and tell interesting things about one another. Talk about jobs, interests, and significant relationships.

Pair up and ask each other: What is the primary thing that, at this stage of your life, you least understand? Talk about some of your thoughts with the group.

The God of Faith
On a scale of 1 to 5 (with 1 being not close at all and 5 being very close), what kinds of activities make you feel closest to God? Reading the Bible? reading particular books? listening to music? sitting in silence? doing something helpful? praying? attending a religious service? other?

The guy dropped the course, but I've always thought about that day in class. I'm more comfortable with things that can be explained rather than things you accept through faith without proof. On the other hand, I'm a Christian—more or less. I was baptized. I go to church on the major holidays. I pray quite a bit. But how can I know that Christianity is true? If God ever spoke to me through the Bible or some other way, how would I know it was God?

HOW DO WE KNOW IT'S TRUE?

As we go through life, we have to take a lot of things on faith. If you are in love, you hope that the person you love will become your lifelong partner. Will that person always be faithful?

You are interviewing for a job. Will that company remain strong amid economic fluctuations? If not, will you be laid off someday?

You want to have a child. Will that child be healthy? Will that child have troubles along the way?

Some people would say that having faith is safe. In the movie *Finding*

L
O
O
K

CLOSER

How Do We Know It's True?
When you refer to "really religious people," who comes to your mind? Answers might include the Pope, the Rev. Billy Graham, Dr. Martin Luther King Jr., Mother Theresa, or others.

Group the names according to type, for example, "evangelist," "worker with the poor," and so on. What qualities do these people have that make you associate them with relig- ion? If you could trade places with any of these people for a day, who would you choose? Who would you not want to be?

Forrester, the title character wears his socks inside out and notes that in some cultures this practice is a sign of good luck. When asked if he believed that, he says, "No, but it's like prayer. What's the risk?"

Religions have claims to truth that have to be taken seriously. Christianity, for example, offers a close relationship with God through Jesus Christ. It also offers eternal life. How do we earn such a gift? We don't. God offers it free of charge. All we need to do is believe that it is true. However, we are back to the original problem. How do we know it is true?

In the Christian tradition the Bible is the primary source of our knowledge about God. It does not offer the tools of scientific observation. It does offer the God-inspired wisdom of a particular group of people in a particular part of the world as they sought to understand God's nature and God's activity. In a rich variety of materials written and collected over hundreds of years, the open-hearted reader can encounter the God of the Judeo-Christian faith, justice, mercy, love, and salvation.

The Bible sometimes describes God in human terms, using images like a strong arm or holding out hands to save. God cannot be "humanized" in order to be controlled and scrutinized. God is mysterious and beyond complete human observation. Indeed, as we read in Exodus, God is too holy to approach. Yet, in Genesis, God walks with Adam and Eve in the cool evening breezes.

In the Bible, God has different relationships with different people. God speaks through people like Moses and the prophets. God acts to save the people and to reveal God's ways of life through the law. In

Biblical Mysteries
Look up the Bible references in "Bible Studies 101." How does Paul use the word *mystery*? How does the meaning change depending on his context? Look up the word *mystery* in a Bible dictionary or concordance. What are some other ways the word is used in the Bible? Do Greek mystery religions remind you of any contemporary religions or organizations? Which ones? In what ways?

Unpacking the Mystery in *Mystery*

the New Testament, the miracles and teachings of Jesus Christ reveal God's love, mercy, and justice.

The New Testament uses the word *mystery* to refer to religious and spiritual ideas. Interestingly, "the mysteries of God" are things that had been hidden but now are revealed to everyone.

A KNOWN MYSTERY

In Paul's letters, the word *mystery* refers to Jesus. Read Ephesians 3:5-6. Paul had once believed that God related in a special, though not necessarily exclusive, way to the Hebrew people. In ancient Hebrew thought, God was not known through scientific speculation. God made God's self known. The laws of the Torah, starting with the Ten Commandments in Exodus 20 and continuing through Deuteronomy, and the prophets (Isaiah and Jeremiah for example), reveal God's desires and God's words for the benefit of the Hebrew people. In turn, the Hebrew people were called to be a blessing to the rest of the world.

In Jesus, God became a human being who shared all the joys, hurts, loneliness, misunderstandings, and pains of other human beings and who suffered horribly as an executed, falsely accused criminal. Paul resisted Jesus at first. In his view, a crucified messiah was an oxymoron. Finally God revealed to Paul that through Jesus, God provided immeasurable blessing to Jews and to Gentiles, all who were non-Jews.

Paul backed up his convictions with evidence. Gentiles were receiving the same Holy Spirit that had, in ancient times, only empowered special people such as the Hebrew prophets. This

A Known Mystery
Do a word association game. What comes to your mind when you hear the words *Holy Spirit*? Some images may be negative: uncertainties about "speaking in tongues" and the "sin against the Holy Spirit," for example. Some may be positive: God's comfort, peace, counsel, and grace. What do you know at this stage in the study about the Holy Spirit? What comes to your mind when you hear the words *mystery, religious, spiritual*? What do your answers say about your assumptions about faith and religion?

Form groups of two or three. What are some of your favorite mystery authors, movies, or TV programs? Have each person tell about his or her preferences. What thoughts or feelings do you have about using the word *mystery* to describe God?

Spirit provided knowledge and help to people who had, perhaps, never heard of the Jewish religion before. In Christ, God revealed love and blessing to everyone through the Spirit.

WHAT IS THE EVIDENCE?

Julie: I like Paul's interest in evidence. I think I understand what he was talking about. But haven't times changed? In the first century, God was touching the lives of Gentiles. But today, most Christians are already Gentiles, not Jewish converts. I don't see what God is doing today in the first decade of the twenty first century that's as momentous and significant as that. Christian religion seems more staid and uneventful.

Kwame: Here's an idea. Today, maybe we need to look at similar circumstances. In the first century, Jews and Gentiles didn't really relate to each other. Later, whites and blacks in this country didn't relate for years and years. It was a tremendous thing when God brought Jews and Gentiles into fellowship—tremendous enough to "prove" that Jesus was the Messiah.

Anisa: I like that. If we want to prove that God exists, let's look at situations in which people are relating to each other, especially people who wouldn't have associated until God brought them together somehow. Let's look at people

What Is the Evidence?
Write a poem or song lyric directed to God about a time when you did not know what God was doing. Did the situation become clearer later? How?

Write about a time (another time or the same time) when some of your most deeply held ideas where overturned. What happened? Was it an upsetting experience? How did you respond? Where do you think God was in that experience?

Are the feelings you have expressed happy? sad? ambivalent? angry?

Draw a picture of God's overall plan for salvation using crayons, pencils, and poster board or paper. Read Ephesians 3:5-6.
• Why do you think God's mystery of Christ was not known to "former generations" mentioned in verse 5?
• If you were God, would you have planned salvation in this way? Why or why not?
• What do you think might be God's plans for the future?

Designate two people in the group to make plans for a big party that they will host next weekend. Have them make the plans privately while the rest of the group does something else. Then have them return to the group without sharing the plans. What is the group's reaction to these mysterious proceedings?

Then have the whole group make plans for the big party. Which kinds of planning felt the best to the group?

who are supporting and forgiving one another. That's where you'll really see the Spirit working.

WHAT KIND OF "SPIRITUAL" ARE YOU?

Read 1 Corinthians 12:1-11. This is a well-known section of Paul's letter in which Paul tries to warn the congregation about the dangers of being in cliques. The Corinthian Christians were impressed with showy leadership, and they tended to form groups within the church and, at the same time, tolerate serious problems in their midst. New Testament churches were just as human as twenty-first century churches!

In these verses, Paul reminds us that there is diversity in the church. Everyone is blessed with different gifts and abilities, but it is the same Spirit of God who provides these gifts to many different kinds of people. For Paul, this is further evidence that proves the truth of Christ.

Many people are surprised to learn that there are different spiritual types. People are not the same and neither are the ways they respond to faith, spirituality, religion, or kinds of religious art, music, and other expressions of faith. A good book that explains these ideas is *Discover Your Spiritual Type*, by Corinne Ware (Alban Institute, 1995). Based on ideas developed by writer Urban T. Holmes, Ware shows that there are at least four spiritual types:

Head Spirituality. This kind of person likes to think through religious ideas. He or she appreciates theological concepts, thought-

What Kind of "Spiritual" Are You? Rank the following activities according to your favorite ways to learn:
- reading quietly
- having parties
- watching videos
- doing research
- doing crafts
- writing poems
- drawing or painting pictures
- brainstorming with other people
- conducting interviews
- memorizing Scriptures or poems, for example
- silent meditation
- sharing feelings
- directing other people in tasks
- playing learning games with others
- doing a service project
- reading step-by-step instructions
- listening to music
- writing in a journal
- listening to lectures
- writing songs
- doing logical puzzles
- performing a drama or role play

Use the same list and rank them according to your favorite ways to learn and grow spiritually.

provoking sermons, study groups, books, and writing essays and journals. They "get" the Spirit through words.

Heart Spirituality. This kind of person "gets" the Spirit through emotions and emotional experiences. He or she is deeply touched by music, evangelism and testimony, upbeat and spontaneous church services, and internal spirituality.

Mystic Spirituality. A person of a more mystical turn also appreciates internal spirituality. He or she finds spiritual meaning in contemplative, often non-verbal, prayer and in a simple lifestyle. This kind of person is happy to sit silently, waiting for God to speak to the inner, intuitive self.

Kingdom Spirituality. This kind of person finds God through action. They want to see the world become a better place. They want to work for some idea and to enlist others to strive for the same vision.

BETWEEN FRIENDS

Anthony: That's exactly right! I'm a "heart" person. I love praise choruses and upbeat music! Michael, maybe you ought to try your aunt's church.

Michael: I don't want to try my aunt's church! Her church is too hyper. And I hate praise choruses.

Anthony: Are you saying you don't want to praise the Lord?

Kasie: He wasn't saying that at all, Anthony! You're sounding like the people that made me leave church in the first place!

Between Friends
Discuss how you know God. One way in which people know God is through the Bible. Other answers might be through prayer, sacraments, life experiences, reading, doing good, listening to sermons, getting in touch with one's emotions, and doing creative things.

Make a list of the answers that the group provides. Which ones are primarily individual in nature? Which ones are primarily social? Which ones are combinations of the two?

SPIRITUAL GROWTH

Have you ever felt "put off" by someone else's religion or felt that that person did not understand you? Did they seem too cerebral, too emotional, too detached, or too aggres-

Spiritual Growth
Who were the people in your life who influenced your religious outlook the most? Were these people positive or negative influences? Could you say they were really "in touch" with God? How so? What kinds of people were they (Sunday school teachers, college professors, former roommates, significant others, relatives, acquaintances)? Were they stereotypically "pious" people or not?

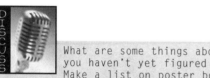

What are some things about God you haven't yet figured out? Make a list on poster board or a chalkboard. Answers might include, "Why did God let [someone important to me] die?" "Why does God let bad things happen?" "Where is God?" "Does God answer prayers?" or "Why does God answer some prayers and not others?" or even "Does God love life on other planets?" or "Why did God make so many insects?"

Into the World
Read aloud this doxology: "O the depth of the riches and wisdom and knowledge of God! How unsearchable are his judgments and how inscrutable his ways! 'For who has known the mind of the Lord? Or who has been his counselor? Or who has given a gift to him, to receive a gift in return?' For from him and through him and to him are all things. To him be the glory forever" (Romans 11:33-36).

sive and guilt inducing? One reason for your reaction may be that you are simply a different spiritual type. Similarly, have you ever disliked a worship service that seemed too liturgical and intellectual? Or, on the other hand, have you felt uncomfortable in a worship service that was too spontaneous, lively, and loud?

Your reaction does not mean there is something wrong with you. True, some people may have to modulate their spiritual type in order not to be judgmental toward others. We all have different spiritual paths. Part of spiritual growth is figuring out what speaks to you, what opens you to the movements of the Spirit, and who the people are that are close to you spiritually.

INTO THE WORLD

In the New Testament, *mystery* refers to something positive and revealed rather than something negative and unknown. God's mystery is Christ, through whom God gives the Spirit to people in order that they might experience joy, comfort, wisdom, and blessing. God's Spirit brings people together into new kinds of fellowship.

In Romans 9–11, Paul considered a difficult problem: Jews and Gentiles in God's plan of salvation. Instead of coming to a definite, logical conclusion, he ended his discussion with words of praise for God's mysterious ways.

God's Spirit works in people's lives in many different ways. Because we are different kinds of people, God speaks to us according to who we are and where we are along our individual spiritual journeys.

GOD'S MYSTERIOUS PRESENCE

This session explores God's presence in the mysteries of pain, death, and the end of time.

DECISIONS, DECISIONS

As young adults, many of you are deciding what you would like to do in your lives, what dreams you would like to pursue, and what responsibilities you would like to shoulder. Some of these may include

- marriage
- college or graduate school
- new job, new career
- purchase of a house
- plan for financial future

Such decisions invite a question that, unfortunately, may be difficult to answer: What will the future bring? Other questions may come to mind: Will I make the right decisions? Will I choose the right person to marry? Will I enjoy the career I choose? Will I plan correctly? What "curve balls" will life pitch to me? Amid life's unpredictable joys and sorrows, how does one grow spiritually?

START
Greet one another, and welcome any newcomers. Invite participants to tell about a goal or dream they wish to pursue. Ask one another for prayers and support, for yourself or others.

DISCUSS
Decisions, Decisions
What is the biggest decision you are facing at this time of your life? To whom, if anyone, will you look for help in making this decision? How have you arrived at big decisions previously in your life?

BIG QUESTIONS

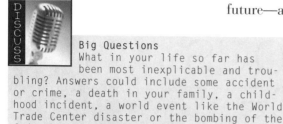

Big Questions
What in your life so far has been most inexplicable and troubling? Answers could include some accident or crime, a death in your family, a childhood incident, a world event like the World Trade Center disaster or the bombing of the federal building in Oklahoma City, or some other personal or public circumstance. How do you think God was present in that circumstance? Or do you think God actually was present at all? Why or why not?

Anisa: Sometimes I wish I knew the future—at least some things. It would be nice to be able to prepare for something that's on the horizon.

Kasie: I couldn't disagree more! If I had known in advance that my mom was going to have breast cancer, life would have been miserable.

Anthony: On the other hand, if you knew something in advance, you could avoid that situation or try to change it; like that TV show, *Early Edition*, where the guy gets tomorrow's newspaper today then goes around saving people. But I'm not sure the future is something we even could know in advance. What if the future is all unwritten? What if the future is what we make it day to day?

Michael: That seems to fly in the face of what the Bible says: God knows the time and circumstances of Jesus' return.

Julie: Yes, but does that mean God knows everything that's going to happen way in advance? Did God, at the beginning of time, decide that Anisa was going to raise this question and we all start discussing it? If so, God's micromanaging, in my humble opinion!

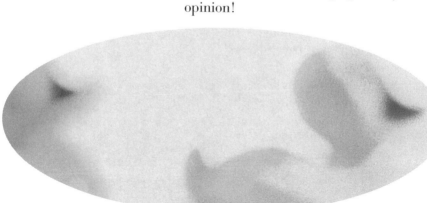

Kwame: I've got ideas about all this. If we knew everything in advance, we'd never face any challenges that make us better people. We're stronger when we have to solve our problems on a day-by-day basis.

The Age-Old Question
Read Luke 13:1-5. Jesus says that people who suffer tragedy do not die because they have done something wrong. Everyone sins. The fact that tragic things happen may stimulate us to consider our own lives. How does Luke 13:1-5 apply to situations you have experienced?

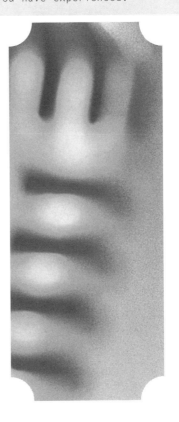

THE AGE-OLD QUESTION

Most of us have, at one time or another, pondered why things happen the way they do. Some people just seem to have bad luck. They go around as if a little rain cloud floats over their heads. There are others who seem to face very few problems in their lives.

We all know stories that call attention to the seeming unpredictability of life, the apparently random way good fortune and misfortune befall people. Some will say that God sends or allows misfortune in order to teach us things. Others will say that God would not send terrible misfortune, but God helps us when trouble happens.

KATRINA'S JOURNAL

"I hear people complaining about how tough life is. I say, 'Get over it. Life's tough for everybody!'

"But sometimes even I get mad at God when trouble comes to people who can't handle it. My grandpa couldn't boil water; but Grandma died, leaving him all alone. He was completely lost without her and never understood why she died. Of course, I have a problem with terrible tragedies—like Columbine or the World Trade Center—that seem to have no reason except evil people getting the upper hand.

"I struggle with how to share the gospel with people. I certainly don't want to say 'Jesus will fix all your problems if you become a Christian.' I've heard preachers preach that way, but to me it just isn't true. What's the good news of Jesus for people who are struggling with decisions and problems?"

SECRETS OF GOD

Daniel had three friends—Hananiah, Mishael, and Azariah. The four youths, Hebrew exiles in Babylon, also went by the Babylonian names of Belteshazzar, Shadrach, Meshach, and Abednego. According to Daniel 1:17, God gave them "knowledge and skill in every aspect of literature and wisdom"; but Daniel "also had insight into all visions and dreams." King Nebuchadnezzar sought interpretation of his troublesome dreams. When Daniel received a vision that explained the king's dream, Daniel sang praise to God.

Read Daniel 2:17-23. Daniel called God the one who "reveals deep and hidden things; God knows what is in the darkness, and light dwells with God" (verse 22). God does not keep things hidden, but "gives wisdom to the wise and knowledge to those who have understanding."

Secrets of God
What are your dreams like? Do you dream in black and white or in color? Do your dreams seem to carry meaning, or are they merely images from your subconscious? How much stock do you place in people's belief that God speaks through dreams?

Bible 101: Apocalyptic Literature
The Greek word *apokalypsis* means "unveiling" or "revealing." Apocalyptic literature is the name for those writings that reveal God's secret, hidden plans, especially concerning the end of time. It emerges from specific historical contexts and offers hope to oppressed people. While apocalyptic literature is diverse, in general it expresses the belief that God will destroy evil and establish God's good realm of mercy and justice. In the Old Testament, the Book of Daniel is an example of apocalyptic writing. Some of the prophets, Isaiah 24-27, for example, also contain elements of apocalyptic writing. In the New Testament, the Book of Revelation is the most obvious Scripture of an apocalyptic nature. Other passages, especially Jesus' sayings recorded in Mark 13, Matthew 24, and Luke 21, express apocalyptic themes. Although the purpose of these writings is to unlock the secrets of God's hidden purposes, the symbolic and often obscure language deters many readers.

According to Daniel, God reveals wisdom to those who are already in a position to understand. God helps those with faith to understand more things and to grow in faith. God gives all people, with or without faith, the space in which they might grow and explore.

TREASURES OF GOD

On the popular television show *The Antiques Roadshow*, people bring their antiques to appraisers who judge the value of the items. Some items, purchased at comparatively cheap prices, turn out to be worth thousands of dollars. One of the most enjoyable reasons to watch this show is seeing people's excitement when they discover that their garage sale vase is worth the price of a new car.

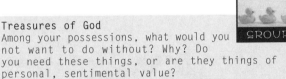

Treasures of God
Among your possessions, what would you not want to do without? Why? Do you need these things, or are they things of personal, sentimental value?

Read 2 Corinthians 4:6-7. What is the treasure to which Paul refers? What are the earthen vessels/jars of clay to which he refers? What kind of "container" do you consider yourself to be: a cracked pot, a Ming vase, a mason jar, a thermos bottle, an old can, or a spray bottle?

Read Colossians 1:24–2:5. Paul writes about "the riches of assured understanding" that believers have, "the knowledge of God's mystery, Christ himself, in whom are hidden all the treasures of wisdom and knowledge" (2:2-3). Paul echoes this conviction in Ephesians 1:13-14.

Paul is not saying that Christ provides "secret knowledge" that is available only to a few; rather, believers have access to knowledge, grace, and blessing. Through Christ we know that God is compassionate, merciful, ready to forgive, and willing to help. Through Christ we know that God is not capricious, vindictive, dissatisfied, or vengeful. We look at what Jesus taught and how he treated people in order to know who God is.

ALL WILL BE CHANGED

Getting to Heaven
Would you depend on God for money matters? help at work or school? protection for you and your family from crime, accident, or natural disaster? guidance for a hard decision? healing from life-threatening illness? If so, what would such dependence actually look like in real life? What are our responsibilities in these matters? What are God's?

One of the classic "future predictions" in the Bible is found in 1 Corinthians 15:50-58. Anyone familiar with the oratorio *The Messiah* will hear Handel's melodies in some of these verses. The resurrection is a mystery, Paul says (verse 51). He could not explain how our bodies—mortal, perishable, and imperfect—will become immortal and imperishable. Nor could he predict the time when "the trumpet will sound, and the dead will be raised" (verse 52). He did know, however, these events will take place because Jesus has already risen from the dead.

The passage comes at the end of the chapter about Jesus' resurrection. In verses 12-34, Paul stressed that Jesus' resurrection was necessary for humankind. Christ is the "new Adam" who brings people to life after the sin of the first Adam brought death to the world (verse 22). Furthermore, our faith depends on the fact that Jesus rose from the dead (verse 17). If Christ did not rise, then people who believe in him are "to be pitied" (verse 19).

When Paul says, "Listen, I will tell you a mystery!" (verse 51), he does not just mean that he does not understand the "physics" of resurrection. True, no one knows how dead people acquire living, immortal bodies that live with God forever. Paul meant that the resurrection has been a secret but is now revealed to everyone. How do we know this secret? Because Jesus has risen from the dead.

Christianity is not just the story of the violent death of a good man. Christianity is not merely a set of morals for people to follow. Christianity tells a secret to everyone. God will bring us to life. Death is no more an enemy, even though death is still real and still brings pain. Death does not have the last word. Jesus has conquered death.

Someone once said that Jesus' resurrection is like the decisive battle of a war. The Allied invasion of Normandy in June 1944 was one such battle. So was the defeat of Lee's army at Gettysburg in July 1863. In both cases, war dragged on, and many people suffered and died, the outcome, however, was assured. So it is with Jesus' victory over death.

KATRINA'S JOURNAL

"While waiting in line at McDonald's®, I was thinking about things that can't be hurried. (Trust me, a long line is the perfect place to think about that!) I may be able to get a burger and some fries in less than ten minutes, but I can't create the Grand Canyon that quickly. I can't make a really good cheese today; it has to age. I can't grow as a person overnight or solve my problems and insecurities with the snap of a finger. Dr. Martin Luther King Jr. had a dream of a free and loving world; he didn't live to see it, but he helped us move in that direction. Christa McAuliffe said she 'touched the future' by teaching, but she'd never know what the future would bring."

STILL QUESTIONS

Along with death and taxes, you could list confusion as one of life's certainties. What decisions should you make? Why does life work out sensibly in some ways and irrationally in other ways?

God lets us in on some of God's secrets. In Jesus, death has been

Still Questions
In the ancient world, people believed that fate, combined with the capricious whims of the gods, directed their lives. The gospel of a loving parent God who ordered their lives and brought them to heaven was a welcomed alternative. How important is it to you that Christ defeated death? How does the idea of eternal life make a difference in your life?

SMALL GROUP

Form groups of two or three. Talk about the following: What do you think existences beyond death will be like? Using a chalkboard or a large piece of paper, list as many aspects as you can. You might think of such things as:

- streets of gold
- people playing harps
- relatives and friends
- God will be visible
- mansions
- plentiful food
- no bad hair days
- every day is sunny
- people can go barefooted

CLOSE

Sit together with friends. Think about the mystery of God's love and presence. After a few moments, close with spontaneous prayers of thanks or requests for yourselves and others.

defeated. In Jesus, God works to guide, help, and sustain us. Not everyone will see this, which is why Paul used the term *mystery*. Through faith we can experience God's help. We know that in Christ, death does not have the last word.

Christianity is sometimes accused of being too "other worldly." In other words, Christians think about going to heaven and neglect important social issues like the environment and justice, for example. In other words, if heaven is your destination, why worry about the world?

Sure, many things in life, including death, will cause us physical and emotional pain. Because of Christ, however, we know that a power greater than ourselves is in control.

We have "elbow room" in which to explore God's mysteries. As Christians, we sometimes have doubts. We do not always have the answers when life deals senseless cards. Wise people have both knowledge and practical know-how. Someone with religious wisdom has "head" knowledge about God and experiences gained through a relationship with God. Such a relationship has plenty of room for questions, mistakes, heartaches, quarrels, and fresh starts.

God works in relationship with us to increase our knowledge, wisdom, and faith; and God works with us according to our special gifts.

THE HOLY SPIRIT

This session explores the idea and reality of God's Spirit.

GETTING INSIDE

What comes to mind when you hear the term *Holy Spirit*?

Some people may have vaguely sinister notions of the Holy Spirit; the word *spirit* has spectral connotations, after all. In Mark 3:28-29, Jesus talked about "the blasphemy against the Holy Spirit" that could never be forgiven. In that passage, Jesus spoke about the kind of constant, deliberate, and perverse resistance to God that would keep a person from experiencing God's grace.

The term *Holy Spirit* also connotes, for some people, "speaking in tongues." In many Pentecostal churches, people speak in unintelligible sounds. They claim that the Holy Spirit, or the Holy Ghost, gives them such power. They believe that the tongues are a sign of God's Spirit present in them.

START

Greet one another and welcome any newcomers. Tell what *Holy Spirit* suggests to you. Ask one another for prayers and support for yourself or others.

CASE STUDY

Getting Inside
If you were describing how the Holy Spirit dwells in you right now, would you say (a) my cup runneth over with God's love; (b) sometimes I feel close to God, and sometimes not very; (c) I'm close to God but I always have to work at the relationship; (d) I don't have a ghost of a chance.

In traditional creedal terms, *Holy Spirit* refers to the third person of the Trinity. Other people think of the Holy Spirit as a comforter and as a helpful presence. Other ways of describing the Spirit are:

- The Spirit is God's very self, God present with us.
- The Spirit makes God real to us.
- The Spirit guides, directs, teaches, admonishes, and loves us.
- The Spirit puts us in the presence of the living Jesus 2,000 years after his earthly life.

Sing a Hymn

Most church hymnals have a variety of songs about the Holy Spirit: "Spirit of the Living God," "Surely the Presence of the Lord," "I'm Goin' a Sing When the Spirit Says Sing," "Every Time I Feel the Spirit," "Holy, Holy, Holy," for example. Check out your church's hymnal and look in the index under "Holy Spirit," "Trinity," "Assurance," "Commitment," "Pentecost," and similar topics. Which are your favorites?

Choose a hymn about the Holy Spirit and sing it. Write your own hymn. What images and ideas would you use for the Holy Spirit?

"The Spirit knows our future," a friend of mine said recently, "so why should we be anxious?" Sometimes there are plenty of reasons to be anxious. Young adulthood can be a time of exploration. You may be thinking about careers or about what you want to do with your life. You may be starting a family or deciding if you want to have children. Many of you are looking at your spiritual lives, too. You may want to discover a faith that is more personally meaningful. You may want to find a church that speaks to you.

The Holy Spirit can and does take an active role in helping to answer life's questions.

AN EXCERPT FROM ANISA'S E-MAIL TO JULIE

"Michael told me about his aunt who speaks in tongues. At her church, they believe that speaking in tongues shows that God's Spirit is present. She keeps inviting Michael to her church, but he doesn't want to go. He showed me 1 Corinthians 14, where Paul talks about speaking in tongues but discounts its importance unless it helps and builds up the congregation.

"I gave him my two cents by saying that he needs to find his own spiritual path and not be forced to choose his aunt's."

Anisa's E-mail to Julie
Read 1 Corinthians 14. *Tongues* means languages (not necessarily known, foreign languages) that people purport to speak through the Spirit's power. What, according to Paul, is the problem with speaking in tongues? What is the true purpose of tongues? Does he approve or disapprove of tongues-speaking?

WHO IS THE HOLY SPIRIT?

The Holy Spirit is not the same as one's soul. The Greek word for soul is *psyche*, which has become an English word in its own right and also the root for the

Who Is the Holy Spirit?
After reading "Bible 101: Breath and Spirit" and the lesson so far, what words express the Holy Spirit best for you? Counselor? mentor? an advocate who is on your side? a good friend? a big, scary force? still very mysterious? other?

Read John 14 and 15, noting especially the references to the Holy Spirit. Put yourself in that situation. How would Jesus' words of goodbye have affected you? What comfort do you derive from his words?

37

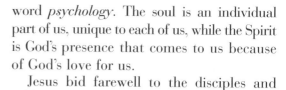

word *psychology*. The soul is an individual part of us, unique to each of us, while the Spirit is God's presence that comes to us because of God's love for us.

Jesus bid farewell to the disciples and told them about the Holy Spirit (John 14:16). He reassured them that while he was about to leave them, someone else would come. "The Advocate, the Holy Spirit, whom the Father will send in my name, will teach you everything, and remind you of all that I have said to you" (verse 26).

The word *advocate* also can mean "counselor." An advocate is someone who takes one's side, who speaks on one's behalf. A counselor is someone to whom we can speak with confidence. A counselor listens to us, helps us reach understanding, and gives us perspective.

AN EXCERPT FROM JULIE'S E-MAIL TO ANISA

"Michael needs to find his own way. My dad admits that he tried LSD back in the '60s. He's lucky to have stopped using drugs before he got busted or worse. He tried Buddhism and TM and New Age, but now he's settled into a church that he likes.

"I like being independent. Maybe that's my problem. I don't really want God or anyone else to tell me what to do. Christians act like they have to say and think certain things and act in certain ways. I don't want to live like a robot, even in the name of religion.

Julie's E-mail to Anisa
Has anyone in your family experimented with consciousness-altering drugs? with Eastern religions? with meditation techniques? with New Age religions? If you need a sense of God's presence, what do you usually do first?

Julie wants the rewards of religion without being confined by rules and expectations. What are the problems with Julie's attitude toward religion? the advantages? What about "organized Christianity" might impede honesty about one's struggles, faults, skeletons in the closet, and so on?

"Sometimes I wouldn't mind a little help. I'd love to have a sense of God's presence, at least once in a while."

THE TRINITY

Christianity speaks of God as Father, Son, and Holy Spirit. The idea of the Trinity is rooted in the Bible. Matthew 28:19 calls for the baptism of new disciples in the name of the Father, the Son, and the Holy Spirit. First Corinthians 12:4-5 clarifies God's oneness in varieties of gifts and services. Paul's words of blessing in 2 Corinthians 13:14 name three activities of God's grace, love, and relationship in terms of Father, Son, and Holy Spirit. The Trinity is not three gods, but rather a way of saying that God relates to people and to creation in three different ways. For example, a woman is one person, but she may be a wife, a mother, and a sister—one person, three different relationships. God creates (Father); God becomes human to save us (Son); and God comes to us as a counselor, comforter, and guide (Spirit).

LOOK CLOSER

The Trinity
List the different roles or characteristics that describe you. Some of your roles might be father or mother, student, employee, son or daughter. Some of your characteristics might be CD collector, mystery novel reader, cat lover. Some of your aspirations might be author-to-be, world traveler, for example.

What illustrations describe how God could be one God but also three different relationships? If you are ambitious, check out a theological dictionary that explains some of the classic theological explanations of the Trinity.

WHAT THE HOLY SPIRIT DOES

SMALL GROUP

What the Holy Spirit Does
What was your all-time best experience in church? What was your all-time worst experience in church? Have you ever attended church and you had no idea what was supposed to be happening? Did anyone help you figure it out? When did you feel pressured to attend church?

A popular church marquee reads, "God wants fruit of the Spirit, not religious nuts!" What is "fruit" of the Spirit? "Fruit" is the result of the Spirit's work in a person's life. Read Galatians 5:16-25. In this passage Paul lists the fruit of the Spirit: "Love, joy, peace, patience, kindness, generosity, faithfulness, gentleness, and self-control" (verses 22-23). He contrasts these with "works of the flesh" and lists several, from the "big" sins—fornication, idolatry, and sorcery—to the "little" sins we usually excuse: envy, anger and jealousy, for example. According to Paul's letters, the word *flesh* does not simply refer to sexuality (which is not itself sinful but can be abused), but to a self-centered, weak human nature. When one is led by the Spirit, Paul says, one can begin to "crucify" one's flesh and, instead, develop the Spirit's fruit.

In Galatians, Paul tells the church that, in Christ, we are not saved by being good people who follow the rules. We are saved only through the power of Christ. That does not mean we are free to do as we please. We are free to accept God's power, the Spirit's power, to help us grow as loving, serving persons.

WHAT THE HOLY SPIRIT GIVES

Read 1 Corinthians 12. In verse 2, Paul says, "When you were pagans, you were enticed and led astray to idols." In ancient Greek religions, followers would become overwhelmed with emotional experiences while worshiping the gods. Paul says if a person is really led by the Spirit of God, he or she confesses Christ as Lord (verse 3).

Paul discusses several gifts of the Spirit: utterance of wisdom, utterance of knowledge, faith, healing, working miracles, preaching (prophecy), discernment of spirits, languages spoken while in a state of religious ecstasy (tongues), and the interpretation of tongues (verses 8-11), as well as teaching and other gifts (verse 28). These different gifts function like parts of the human body; none are dispensable, all function together (verses 14-27). In fact, the way we know the gifts of God's Spirit is that they will always work for the common good through mutual service (12:5, 7; 14:33). For this reason, love is the greatest of God's gifts (13:1-13).

Compare this section to Philippians 4:8-9. Through the Spirit, God creates something new, like an alternative reality. In this alternative reality we love one another, we have peace with one another, and we share our spiritual gifts in order to serve one another.

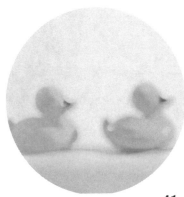

> **Gifts of the Spirit**
> Read Galatians 5:16-25. What are some sins Paul does not mention? What spiritual gifts, if any, did he leave out? In Paul's list of sins, many of us avoid the "big sins" and think we are finished—yet we are still plagued with anger, jealousy, and envy. How does the Spirit heal us of those "little" sins? Use your imagination. (One person suggested that "God healed me of impatience by giving me lots of red lights on the way to work!") How do we produce the fruit of the Spirit?

GROWING SPIRITUALLY

Have you ever sat in church and felt as though you were the only person not getting it? A church service that makes one person feel blessed and happy may leave another person cold and dissatisfied. Whose fault is it? The church's? yours? It may not be anyone's fault. There are different kinds of churches but only one Spirit.

Author Corinne Ware writes that "as a spiritual director, I have noticed that each person exhibits very pronounced and different spiritual needs. This often has seemingly nothing to do with 'maturity'; rather, it

Form two teams of two or three. Think about the moments of your life when you have felt especially close to God. What was different about that moment? How might the Holy Spirit have been directing you?

Worship Together
Sing "Spirit of the Living God" or another song about the Holy Spirit. Pray for each person in your group, and ask God to continue helping him or her to grow spiritual. Thank God for specific things you have learned in these lessons so far. Ask God to continue showing you areas of growth, new insights, and ways to be strong as you go through your life's challenges and tasks.

has to do with an inner-directed and innate spiritual temperament" (*Discover Your Spiritual Type*, page 83). She also says that once we discover what kind of spirituality we are, we can identify our spiritual strengths and capabilities. "You do not need to have the same desires as others. The creator has made you to find your connection to the Holy in a particular way" (page 84). Ware gives the example of one of her friends feeling discontented in church. Finally, he discovered that his spirituality was opposite of the kind of spirituality present at his church. This discovery helped Ware's friend to deal with his discontentedness.

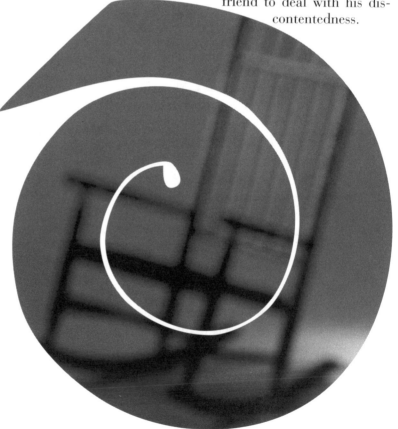

SPIRITUAL FORMATION

This session explores the idea of
spiritual formation as a basis
of one's relationship with God.

HARD WORK

Many things in life require practice or
work. If a student sleeps through classes
and slacks off all semester, he or she will not
do well.

Relationships require work. A successful
marriage involves two people who invest
time and energy to maintain a meaningful
relationship. If little is con-
tributed to the relationship,
the stresses can be enor-
mous. If an old flame shows
up or money problems arise or some other
crisis intervenes, the relationship will not be
strong enough to meet life's challenges.

Introduce yourselves by stating your
name and one activity that you
believe is worthy of hard work.

A writer who wants to be successful must
write regularly, even when he or she is less
than inspired. Every article or chapter may
not be perfect, but it
is in the regular
exercise of writing
that the writer finds
inspiration and is
able to hone the
craft.

Hard Work
List the things that you're good at and
those things that you're not good at. In a
group, compare the lists you have made.
Group your lists according to common
traits, for example, those that require physical
skill, manual dexterity, mental discipline,
patience, or other skills.

A writer once said, "If I weren't writing, I couldn't catch those moments when everything really falls into place."

Athletes practice hard for hours in order to improve their skills. They may not be great every time they play, but they have to play and practice in order to improve. Sometimes practice, ability, and heart come together and cause an athlete to play a fantastic game.

Is religion similar to these examples? The whole idea of spiritual formation suggests that one's faith requires attention and practice. Yet religion is not something you get good at only because you practice. Your practice opens your mind and heart to the one who is really doing all the grace-full work: God.

ЄMЄRGЄNCY Є-MAIL #1

To: Mystery List
From: Anthony

"Hey guys. Last Sunday my pastor talked about spiritual formation. She said you're supposed to do certain things to grow spiritually, but I always thought God made us grow spiritually. I've read Ephesians 2 where Paul says it's 'a gift from God and not of ourselves, lest anyone should boast.' But the pastor left for some annual meeting of clergy and can't answer my questions 'til she gets back. In the meantime, does anyone have any thoughts about this? Do I have to do anything special to grow spiritually, or is God going to do it? What's up with spiritual formation?"

GOD'S UNFAILING LOVE

The Scriptures teach us that we never can earn God's love and favor. God loves us as we are. According to Archbishop Desmond Tutu, "There is nothing you can do that will make God love you less. There is nothing you can do to make God love you more. God's love for you is infinite, perfect, and eternal."

How many times have you felt inferior to someone who seems more spiritual than you? How many times have you thought you needed entrance requirements like a conversion experience, baptism, or some weekend retreat program in order to be a Christian. How many times have you promised God you would do something if only God would bless you? How many times have you thought that God's love decreases each time you fail? God does not withdraw from our account

God's Unfailing Love
Form teams of two or three. Discuss some of
the things you have to do to join a church.
Make a list of things you think are necessary, such as:
  • wearing certain clothes
  • taking regular showers
  • knowing the right people
  • giving a certain amount of money
  • volunteering for certain jobs the pastor wants filled
How close to the truth are your ideas?

SMALL GROUP

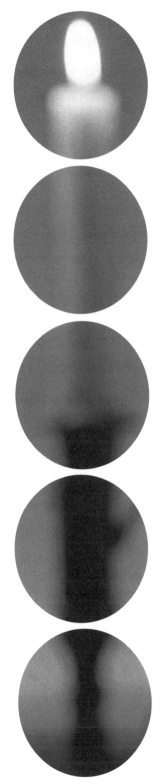

each time we say a curse word or get angry with someone or mess up in some way. Then we worry that our account must be way overdrawn.

Not so. God's love for us is infinite and constant. God's love is completely free. We grow spiritually to please God just as we would please someone we love. Growing spiritually is not about doing something to placate God.

EMERGENCY E-MAIL #2

To: Anthony
From: Michael:

"Hey, Anthony. Paul talks a lot about disciplining yourself spiritually. He talks about presenting your bodies 'as a living sacrifice, holy and acceptable to God, which is your spiritual worship.' That's Romans 12:1. In 1 Corinthians 9:24-27 and Philippians 3:12-14, he talks about 'running the race,' so you can get the prize in 1 Corinthians 9:24, and 'pressing on' and 'straining forward' in Philippians 3:12-14. The prize is the 'heavenly call of God in Christ Jesus.' To me, that sounds like a Christian ought to pursue a disciplined life the way an athlete would."

To: Michael
From: Anthony

"Thanks, Michael. My pastor used the passage from Philippians, too. I guess I'm on the right track then."

FRUIT OF THE SPIRIT

The letter to the Ephesians uses picturesque language to praise God's grace, a grace lavished upon us. Greek mystery religions often had secret rites for certain participants. To Paul, such rites seemed abominable. Why perform religious rites secretly, unless they are shameful? (5:11-12).

Paul also may have been talking about moral actions when he used the expression "unfruitful works of darkness." In Ephesians 5:11, Paul mentioned such works as fornication, impurity, greed, and "obscene, silly, and vulgar talk" (verses 3-4). In Galatians 5:19-23, Paul listed a series of "bad things" and "good things."

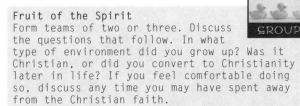

Fruit of the Spirit
Form teams of two or three. Discuss the questions that follow. In what type of environment did you grow up? Was it Christian, or did you convert to Christianity later in life? If you feel comfortable doing so, discuss any time you may have spent away from the Christian faith.

The good things are not what we make ourselves do. Rather, they are results or fruit of the Holy Spirit's presence in our lives. The list includes "love, joy, peace, patience, kindness, generosity, faithfulness, gentleness, and self-control" (verses 22-23).

For many people, there is a discernible line between their old, pre-Christian lives and their new lives in Christ. Ephesians 5:8 talks about this in terms of darkness and light. People may point to the miraculous intervention of God into their lives. They sobered up or got clean. They overcame some problem or trouble. However, Paul does not say that everyone has to have accrediting experiences like that. All of us have to decide, usually many times in our lives, to let the Spirit work in us. That is where spiritual formation comes in. We continue to struggle with our old selves, even in a new, Christian context. But there is a difference. Now we are assured that God is with us.

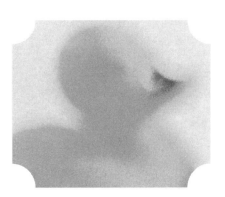

EMERGENCY E-MAIL #3

To: Anthony
From: Kwame

"The Bible talks about spiritual discipline, but what about the thief on the cross? He didn't do a thing to get to heaven except

---

Spiritual Formation

acknowledge Jesus. Paul says in Galatians that there are no requirements to being a Christian—not circumcision, not anything—and he was seriously upset that people would suggest otherwise!

"There's a story in Matthew 20:1-16 that also deals with reward for work. In this story the workers were all paid the same thing, no matter what time they showed up to work. If that happened at my company, I might be a little upset. I guess that just goes to show that God is so generous that he will bless those who work for a long time *and* those who show up at the very last minute. God doesn't bless us because we work hard and impress him, as if he's some supervisor doling out merit pay. God's love is everything; our efforts are nothing."

To: Kwame
    From: Anthony
    "Now I'm more confused than ever!"

LITTLE KID JESUS, RIGHT AT HOME

Think back to when you were a child attending church. Did you ever get stuck at church and could not go home because your parents made you stay? Luke 2:41-52 shows the opposite problem: Jesus felt at home in the Temple, and he did not want to go with his parents! Mary and Joseph assumed that Jesus was with other relatives and

Emergency E-mail #3
Read Matthew 20:1-16. When was a time you were treated unfairly? What happened? How did the situation turn out?

Do a role play. Gather the group in a line. Have one person be the "boss." Depending upon how many people you have, let the boss say to the first person: "You've worked twelve hours, here is your $100. To the next person: "You've worked ten hours, here is your $100." To the last person, "You showed up two minutes before quitting time, here is your $100." What is the reaction of the various group members to all this "equal pay"?

Kids in Worship
Role play a family going to church or synagogue. Have someone in your group pretend he or she is a single parent, and have one or two group members pretend they are children. Perform different skits involving different age groups of children—from very young to elementary age to teenagers. What complaints do the "children" make? What makes them want to attend worship? Try the role play with two parents instead of one. How do the dynamics change?

travelers, so they set out for Nazareth. After a day, however, they could not find him and returned to Jerusalem. Imagine their feelings of panic and self-accusation.

Finally Joseph and Mary found Jesus in the Temple sitting among the teachers and asking questions. Sometimes the religious teachers are portrayed negatively, as if they were too righteous for everyone else. Not so. Apparently they had been feeding and caring for Jesus and putting him to bed at night for three days. They must have enjoyed his company. Meeting in the Temple, the teachers would have been discussing the religious laws as well as the oral traditions of the rabbis. Jesus had know-ledge of these things, even at a young age.

Jesus' parents chided, "Why have you treated us like this?" He answered, "Did you not know that I must be in my Father's house?"

Jesus found the Temple and its ceremonies spiritually helpful, even as a 12-year-old child.

The First Christians

Do a role play about newly converted first-century Christians. The Christians of the early church only had the Old Testament and the Apocrypha for their Bible. Pass out Bibles with rubber bands around the New Testament so that you cannot open that section. What would you study to learn about Jesus? Look at Numbers 21:8-9; Deuteronomy 18:15-22; Psalms 22, 69; Isaiah 43:18-21, 52:13-53:12; Ezekiel 18:31, 36:26; Zechariah 12:10, 13:7-9. What could you learn about Jesus from these Scriptures? What other Scriptures would help? What religious activities would you practice?

Read Acts 2:37-42. Would you be willing to share your possessions with one another? Would you want to support one another for the indefinite future? Why or why not?

THE FIRST CHRISTIANS

Read Acts 2:37-42. Peter had been addressing a large crowd gathered at Jerusalem for the Jewish holiday Shavuot, also called Pentecost. He told them, "Repent, and be baptized every one of

Spiritual Formation

and be baptized every one of you in the name of Jesus Christ so that your sins may be forgiven." To us this may sound like the kind of message you would hear from a preacher shouting from the street corner. For Peter's audience, though, this was a brand-new message.

The text states that nearly 3,000 people were baptized that day, after which people "devoted themselves to the apostles' teaching and fellowship, to the breaking of bread and the prayers." Remember that at that time there was no "church" as we think of church today. People gathered in their homes for fellowship and instruction. Often they shared a community meal and then the Lord's Supper (1 Corinthians 11:17-34). Their Scriptures consisted of the collection of writings we call the Septuagint, or the Old Testament, plus the writings of the Apocrypha. The early Christians studied these Scriptures to understand who Jesus was and to understand what God was doing in their lives. God was several steps ahead of them, of course, so the early Christians were playing catch up on the wonderful things God had done. "Spiritual formation" is like that. We are trying to catch up with what God has done and is doing in our lives.

INTO THE WORLD

Into the World
Have someone read aloud Ephesians 3:20-21. Think about what God is doing in your life right now. After the passage is read, tell others in the group what God is doing in your life.

Do you think that God is doing something in your life but you are not always sure what? Spiritual formation is not about being overly pious. Spiritual formation is more about putting yourself in a position to recognize God's action in your life. God works in our lives for more than our private happiness. God works in order that we might grow and reach out to others in love.

WHAT ARE SPIRITUAL DISCIPLINES?

This session examines several practices that help us connect with God.

WHAT'S THE DIFFERENCE?

What happens when you become a Christian? Some people have emotional experiences that serve as a discernible turning point. Such experiences, however, do not guarantee long-term spirituality. Plenty of people come forward at evangelistic crusades but do not sustain a lifelong, vital relationship with God. Yet, many people do. What makes the difference?

Some grow up in Christian households and remain Christian all their lives. They did not have a conversion experience, yet they have sustained a lifelong relationship with Christ. Others with the same kind of Christian childhood later leave the church. Perhaps they return; perhaps they don't. What makes the difference?

Some religious people are hard to love. They are faithful churchgoers. They tithe and pray; but they are spiteful, critical,

> **START**
> Greet one another and welcome any newcomers. Offer a quick update on life since you last met. Tell about an exercise regimen, diet, or other discipline that you practice or wish to practice.

sneaky—you name it! Yet some of our non-Christian friends, who never attend church, are kind, loving, and honest. What makes the difference?

BECOMING A CHRISTIAN

Becoming a Christian means simply to accept the love that God already has for you through Christ. Once a writer was asked when he became a Christian. He replied, "At Calvary." When you become a Christian, you do not change God's mind from hatred to love. You acknowledge that God has already displayed great love through the death and res-

Becoming a Christian
Read John 3:16. Think about what John 3:16 actually says: Eternal life comes to those who believe in Jesus. What, if anything, challenges you or makes you curious about this Scripture? What does the Scripture say to you about God?

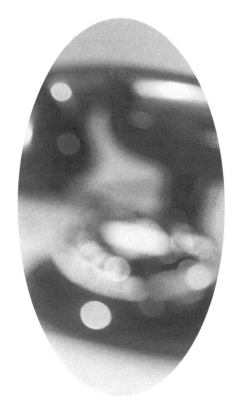

urrection of Jesus. Through that acknowledgement, you embark on life as it was meant to be: oriented around God's love in service to one another. God's love through Christ becomes a guiding principle and a source of power for you.

Accepting Christ—whether as a child or an adult—does not change you permanently, just as saying "I love you" to someone does not result in a lifetime relationship. Relationships such as friendship and marriage require time and attention. Relationship with God needs attention and nourishment in much the same way.

Being a Christian and being a good, moral person may not be the same thing. Many wonderful people are not Christian, and some Christian people, intentionally or not, have terrible qualities. Many Christians fail morally. Let's face it, we all have good and bad qualities. We practice spiritual disciplines in order to allow our relationship with God to change us in positive ways.

The term *spiritual discipline* sounds harsh. God does not bark at us, "Drop and give me twenty!" However, being a Christian does take self-discipline. No one forces you to go to church. No one demands that you pray. You have to want to practice such disciplines. Something special about your time with God keeps you coming back. Something about prayer is satisfying and meaningful to you.

START WITH PRAYER

When you become a Christian, or when you return to the faith after a time away, it is difficult to know what to do. The Bible talks about prayer, fasting, love, and worship; but the formula is not spelled out for us. There are no customized instructions like a set of directions for assembling a stereo system. No list explains precisely how each person should be spiritual. That is the challenge and the joy of growing in one's faith.

Prayer is simply being present in relationship with God. Sometimes it may mean talking to God, and sometimes it may mean listening to God. Prayer can be formal or it can be spontaneous. In all ways of praying we honestly offer ourselves, our thoughts, and our feelings to God. For examples of sincere prayers, read the Psalms. The emotions of the psalmists range from joy to dispair, from fear and anxiety to confidence and affirmation. Thoughts and feelings are offered with honesty.

SMALL GROUP

Start With Prayer
Form teams of two or three and discuss the following: How do you pray? While on the run? once in a while? during quiet times? When you pray, how much of your prayer is talking to God, and how much is listening to what God might be saying?

How does God speak to you? The voice of conscience? the advice of friends? through the Bible? serendipitous encounters? How does God guide you and help you? How would you like for God to guide you and help you?

THE PRAYER OF JESUS

In Matthew 6:1-21, Jesus gives a fresh spin on old religious practices. Pray in the style of the Disciples' Prayer, says Jesus.

The Prayer of Jesus
Read Matthew 6:1-21. For many the
prayer of Jesus, also known as
the Lord's Prayer, has become a rote recitation.
Think about the prayer line-by-line. How much of
it is asking God for things? What are you asking
God for? How much of the prayer is praise?
Compare your own prayers with the Lord's Prayer.
How similar or dissimilar are your prayers with
this one? For fun, make your own prayer model—
"The _____ (fill in your own name here)
Prayer"—that emphasizes your own concerns.

Usually we do not even think about the words when we pray this prayer. Jesus says: "Pray in this way," which does not necessarily mean "pray these particular words." Para-phrasing the prayer reveals some of its meanings. First, acknowledge that God is holy. Pray for wisdom and clarity into God's desires. Pray that God will provide everyday needs for ourselves and for others. Pray that you can forgive others so that you can become open to God's love and forgiveness for you. Pray that God helps you in those times when you face good and bad choices.

Prayer is offered to God; it is not given to impress others. Do not put yourself on a stage so that people can appreciate you and your prayers. Instead, pray in secret where God can hear and respond to your need.

MANY SPIRITUAL DISCIPLINES

In his book, *The Spirit of the Disciplines* (Harper & Row, 1988), Dallas Willard identifies different spiritual disciplines. His list points to the reality that different people respond to different disciplines. When we find a discipline that works for us, we need to remember that other people may prefer other disciplines.

Solitude and silence are interrelated disciplines. When we are alone and it is quiet, we may begin to feel insecure. Company, television, music, and other things can distract us; but solitude accompanied by silence can help us get in touch with God and with our own inner conflicts.

Fasting, which is giving up food for a certain length of time, is another discipline. When he first began his ministry, Jesus fasted in the wilderness for forty days. Fasting for long periods of time usually takes practice, but giving up food—even if it is just breakfast and lunch—reminds us of our dependence on God. God gives us many other blessings in addition to food. The temporary hunger pangs experienced during a fast may remind you of the actual needs of hungry people in the world. You can become more sensitive to the hurts of other people.

Other disciplines include frugality and chastity. Willard writes that the love of money, rather than money itself, is a source of temptation. Reducing some of our expenses is a way to remind ourselves of God's help.

According to Willard, our sexuality is part of our God-given nature. Our sexuality can take center stage, but our spirituality orients our sexuality the same as it orients the way we handle our finances, our use of time, and other aspects of our lives. These are disciplines of abstinence. You are "training" yourself spiritually by giving up something temporarily.

Another discipline, voluntary exile or "keeping watch." Keeping watch is to abstain from sleep in order to devote oneself to spiritual practices, and this discipline is less common today, according to Willard.

Some of the disciplines involve engagement or doing things rather than giving up things. Although keeping a journal is not a traditional discipline, many people enjoy

Many Spiritual Disciplines
Form teams of two or three. Assign different spiritual disciplines to each group. Have the groups write scripts to TV commercials that would convince people how unbelievably wonderful a particular spiritual disciplines is. Use your imagination and sense of humor. Discuss these questions:

Should Christians try all the disciplines at different times of their lives? Or should they instead, find the discipline that meets their spiritual needs? Explain your answer. What should you do if someone else recommends a discipline from which you do not think you would get much benefit?

SMALL GROUP

recording their thoughts, prayers, and experiences.

Worship and fellowship are disciplines of engagement. Serving other people through participation in church or in a social program is another popular spiritual discipline. Willard suggests shopping occasionally in a store in a poorer part of town as a means of service.

Celebration or cultivating a sense of happiness at God's goodness is another discipline. Deuteronomy 14:23-29 demonstrates how pilgrims on their way to Jerusalem were to use their tithe for enjoyment and celebration.

Bible study is a discipline. A person sets aside a regular time to study the Scriptures. You may have heard some people say, "Don't go to the commentaries. Go to the Bible!" However, the Bible is not always clear in its meanings, and not every interpretation that we make comes straight from the Holy Spirit. Good commentaries can clarify difficult passages and put Scriptures in context; and people with whom we study the Bible can, through discussion, help us have a clearer meaning of what the Bible is saying.

BETWEEN YOU AND GOD

Read Matthew 6:1-21. The Jewish tradition stresses purity of heart and action whenever one worships God. Following religious rules is not as important as your love for God and for others. Jesus returned to that emphasis in his teaching in the Sermon on the Mount.

Giving alms, or giving to charity, was considered an important act of religion. However, Jesus warned that we should not "sound a trumpet" (6:2) to announce our giving. You may know of people who like to make a big deal out of their contributions. It is as if they have hired a brass band to strike up a fanfare whenever they drop money into the offering plate! Jesus taught that we should give alms in secret so that only God will know how much we have given.

Jesus says, Center your life on "treasures in heaven" rather than "treasures on earth" (6:20-21). There are many books on the market that show people how to make lots of money. The problem is that if you are overly concerned about money, your heart is on money.

About fasting, Jesus said that we should "not look dismal" and "disfigure" our faces, drawing attention to ourselves. (6:16). Picture someone with his or her face scrunched up, maybe a hand to a growling stomach, saying, "Look at me, I'm so spiritual!" What a silly image! Jesus told his followers to wash their faces and put oil on their heads. Today Jesus might say, "Take a shower and put on fresh deodorant."

Spiritual disciplines are personal. The times you are trying to be closer to God, you must focus on God rather than on the impression you make on others.

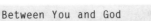

Between You and God
Read Matthew 6:1-21. Draw caricatures of people who make a big show of their spirituality. For example, you might draw a person with a bullhorn shouting, "LOOK EVERYBODY! I'M TITHING!" or a person who switches on an "APPLAUSE" sign whenever he sings a solo in church.

As you read the passage, consider your own Christian walk. What is the difference between "parading your piety" and witnessing to Christ through the things you do?

SPIRITUAL GROWTH

Learning to grow spiritually takes trial and error. You must discover for yourself which spiritual disciplines help you experience God's presence.

SMALL GROUP

Form teams of two or three. In your teams tell about the practices that help you or that might help you feel closer to God.

Modern culture does not help much with its emphasis on quantification; our churches fall into the same trap. Task-oriented pastors try to get us to read the Bible more, to

What Are Spiritual Disciplines?

pray more, to give more, and to volunteer more—as if the church were a company with a quota to meet. Is it more spiritual, for example, to pray an hour a day instead of 30 minutes? Is a congregation with lots of "worker bees" more spiritual than one without? Do you become more spiritual volunteering to teach the 4-year-old children's Sunday school class that you do not enjoy just because the church needs teachers, rather than doing something you love, like singing in the choir? Good disciplines that encourage spiritual growth emerge from your unique identity, gifts, and preferences for relating to God.

INTO THE WORLD

We should be careful in evaluating our need for spiritual disciplines. For many of us, not praying is easier than making the effort to pray. Spiritual activities sometimes break us out of our comfort zones. We need to figure out when we are being led to new areas of growth, when we need to cast off unproductive activities, and when we are just being lazy.

If the church fails you in this regard, don't give up. People experience God through words, emotions, deep inner and intuitive experience, or through social action. Think honestly of what really excites you about spirituality and its varied practices. To what kinds of spiritual growth experiences might God be leading you?

Into the World
Pray together. Pray silently for one another's needs and for one another's spiritual growth. Pray silently that each one can find a "niche" in which to grow spiritually. Give thanks for God's unconditional love made known to us in Jesus.

HOW AM I SUPPOSED TO WORSHIP?

This session examines the meaning of worship as a way to praise God and to receive from God.

PEOPLE WHO ENCOUNTERED GOD

Moses was working hard one day when he encountered a bush that blazed but did not burn up. From this bush, God told Moses to tell Pharaoh to release the Hebrews from slavery. Moses, instead, gave God excuses for why he should not speak to Pharaoh. Finally Moses stopped asking God to send someone else (Exodus 3:1–4:17).

Isaiah considered himself "a man of unclean lips." One day, as he worshiped in the Temple, angels (actually frightening-looking "seraphs") appeared to him, announced the forgiveness of his sins, and gave him a task assigned by God (Isaiah 6:1-8). Unlike Moses, Isaiah was willing and ready.

After the group assembles, share highlights of your lives since the last time you met. Offer in prayer any concerns or needs. Leaf through your church's hymnal and sing or read together a favorite hymn.

Elijah performed a great miracle on God's behalf (1 Kings 18); but to his chagrin, he became a fugitive (19:1-3). Where was God, now that he, God's servant, was in

trouble? Elijah finally heard God's voice, not in spectacular events, but in "a sound of sheer silence" (verse 12). God told him to quit whining because it was not all about Elijah. There were others who served God, too (verses 1-18).

Zechariah was serving as a priest in the Temple when an angel appeared to him and announced, "You're going to be a father!" (Luke 1:5-20). Not long after, Simeon and Anna, who were faithful worshipers at the Temple for many years, finally saw what they had long hoped to see: the Lord's Messiah (2:25-38).

Paul was persecuting Christians when, suddenly, the risen Christ met him on the road and changed his life (Acts 9:1-9).

Cleopas and a fellow traveler, on their way to Jerusalem, encountered a man who talked to them about the Bible and Jesus. Only when the men shared bread and wine did they recognize the stranger as the risen Lord (Luke 24:13-35).

WHAT IS WORSHIP?

Unlike the infomercial miracle products that promise to make us prettier, healthier, wealthier, or more organized, spiritual disciplines are not designed to be a quick fix to better spirituality. Instead, they are to be built into our lives in a meaningful way to help us grow spiritually–over time, not overnight.

As one of the disciplines, worship puts us in the place and in the frame of mind in which God can speak to us. Worship helps us allow God to work in our lives.

In worship we place ourselves in a particular space. We participate in ritual, music, prayer, and hearing God's word. Through these activities, we acknowledge that God is our Lord, Savior, Helper, Creator, and Sustainer. As in the Disciples' Prayer, we ascribe honor and praise to God. We do not flatter God so that God will help us. Instead, in prayer we are responding to God in love and gratitude.

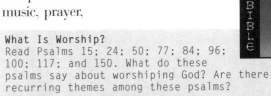

What Is Worship?
Read Psalms 15; 24; 50; 77; 84; 96; 100; 117; and 150. What do these psalms say about worshiping God? Are there recurring themes among these psalms?

Read Psalm 150 again. Raid the choir room for instruments, or borrow children's instruments from the Sunday school department. Praise God in a joyous and spontaneous way. How does it feel to praise God with loud instruments? Does anyone in your church complain about the commotion?

IRREVERENT JOURNAL ENTRY 1

"Religious pundits say that worship is praise and honor to God and that we worship out of love. So why is my parents' church so rote and monotonous? The minister's been there forever! Talk about stale! I leave church wanting to sing the witch's soldiers' song from *The Wizard of Oz*. Don't even get me started on the sermon!"

You Can't Go Home Again
Form teams of two or three. After reading "Irreverent Journal Entry 1," think about the church you attended as a child. If you have a "childhood church," what does it feel like to return there? Talk about some of your experiences with the group.

DIFFERENT STYLES, DIFFERENT TRADITIONS

Religious traditions and different congregations within traditions emphasize a variety of aspects of worship. There are churches that place preaching at the center of worship. Sermons are contemporary explanations of the meaning of a particular portion of Scripture. A sermon may be a homily, a topical lecture, or an ethical or moral theme. Ideally, the minister will preach carefully, prayerfully, and with a deep sensitivity to the needs of the people.

The typical worship service includes one to three passages from the Bible. If a sermon is preached, it is based on these Bible passages, and in theory, the music of the service relates to the Scriptures and the sermon.

Some worship services are "liturgical," or highly structured according to hymns and Scriptures. In some churches, congregations read creeds (ancient statements of belief).

Hymns range from "old fashioned" hymns from the 1700s and 1800s or earlier to more contemporary hymns. In many cases, the contemporary songs originated from Christian recording artists of the past two or three decades, and span many musical genres (country, rap, rock, rhythm and blues, and pop).

LOOK CLOSER

Different Styles, Different Traditions

Frank Mead, Samuel Hill, and Craig Atwood have written a popular book on different Christian traditions called *Handbook of Denominations in the United States* (11th Edition, Abingdon Press, 2001). Study some of the descriptions of the denominations, beginning with the "big" ones (Catholic, Methodist, Presbyterian, Lutheran, Episcopal, Baptist). Notice how many different versions exist of the more well-known denominations as well as how many smaller Christian groups there are. What is appealing to you about different denominations?

Find in your church's hymnal (or another source) the section containing creeds. Read the Apostles' Creed, the Nicene Creed, and the affirmations of faith. What words touch you more deeply?

SACRAMENTS

Worship services sometime include the sacraments. The sacraments practiced in most protestant traditions are those commanded by Christ. They use physical elements (water, bread, and wine) to express God's saving act for us in a specific way. God acts apart from the sacraments, but we recognize that God is at work in the sacraments. Although the Roman Catholic and Orthodox denominations recognize seven sacraments, baptism and the Eucharist are called dominant sacraments; that is, they were specifically commanded by Christ. The other five are called ordinal sacraments. Most other Christians consider baptism and the Eucharist sacraments and call the other observances ordinances.

The Eucharist, or the Lord's Supper, is the sharing of bread and wine as symbols of Christ's body and blood. In eating the bread and drinking the wine, we remember Christ's death and, invisibly, Christ's life comes to us. The word *eucharist* comes from a Greek word meaning "thank you." We thank God for Christ because he died so that each of us can live forever. Some denominations use only wine; others insist that grape juice be used. The Roman Catholic Church also requires unleavened bread; Orthodoxy requires leavened bread. Despite these differences, the essential point of the Eucharist is to recognize that Christ is present with us when we break the bread and share the cup.

The Lord's Supper can be observed daily, once a week, once a month, or once every three months—depending on the con-

Sacraments
What were holidays like in your family? For Paul, sharing the Lord's Supper, and sometimes a group meal, was an important occasion for celebrating Christ's presence. How could we prepare people to become more receptive to Christ on such occasions?

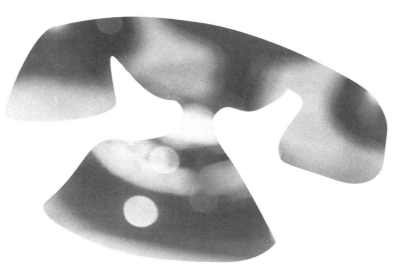

gregation or denominational custom. The Bible does not stipulate how frequently the Lord's Supper should happen.

Baptism is the use of water to signify that the person is a member of God's people. Some churches submerge persons completely in baptism. Other ancient forms include sprinkling or pouring water on the persons being baptized. Some traditions require persons to have reached the age of conscience before being baptized. The dominant practice provides for baptizing infants as well.

Some churches stress that baptism washes away our sins. Other churches say that baptism is an act of obedience and has no effect on the person being baptized.

Baptism happens only once in your life. It is not considered appropriate to be baptized more than once (although some churches do not recognize infant baptism as legitimate and insist on adult baptism when joining their denomination). Baptism is not repeated because it is not something we do but something God does for us. To be baptized again is to say that God did not act in the first baptism.

WHAT DO YOU THINK?

There are varieties of worship among different congregations and denominations. One can make further distinctions based on

Connie Ware's spiritual inventory in her book, *Discover Your Spiritual Type*.

- Is the worship intellectual, planned-out, and doctrinal?
- Is the worship spontaneous, emotional, and centered on the holiness of one's life?
- Does the worship use silence and inward prayer? Is it centered on "being in the presence of God"?
- Does the worship stress service, social involvement, and justice?

As you seek deeper spiritual growth in your life, part of your journey will be identifying the kind of worship that speaks best to you. Worship is about more than choosing what we like. Our worship must also be faithful to God? What kind of worship enables us to be faithful to God? Remember that worship also is *being with other people*. There is a place for solitude along the spiritual journey, but in worship we demonstrate our commonality with other worshipers. We strive to be "the body of Christ," according to the apostle Paul.

What Do You Think?
Read Isaiah 58:1-14. What does God want in our worship? For God, what is false worship, and what is true worship? How do our relationships reflect our relationship with God?

If available, read Chapter 4 of *Discover Your Spiritual Type*, by Connie Ware. How do you relate your own spiritual "type" to Isaiah's caution concerning true worship?

IRREVERENT JOURNAL ENTRY 2

"Here we go again. Mr. Religious Pundit Lesson Author says that worship happens in a community. Easier said than done. I grew up in a small town where everyone knew everything about everyone else. Back home I'll always be "Bill and Helen's granddaughter." I don't feel accepted for who I really am. Bill and Helen's granddaughter, after all, shouldn't be pierced and

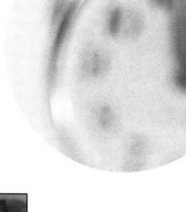

tattooed! Now I live in a city, and I don't know many people. I attend a Sunday school class, but I'd be a fool to open up to people I don't really know.

"I feel very spiritual, maybe even peaceful and prayerful, when I skip church. I go to my favorite bookstore and browse the books with other church-skippers. Why can't I call that 'worship'?"

WHY CHURCH?

Church is more than a place to get together with people, more than a place to get a peaceful, positive feeling. Fellowship and peacefulness can be had in other places, too. Congrega-tions, being made up of human beings, can fall far short on pro-viding peace or fellowship. Plenty of good people do not go to church, and plenty not-so-good people never miss a church service. The point of church attendance, however, is not to prove our goodness.

When we worship together, God's pres-ence can become real to us. We direct our minds and our selves toward God, both in praise and in need. We acknowledge who God is, we acknowledge that God loves us dearly, and we seek to know more about God. We may even feel over-whelmingly happy, and that, too, is a sign of God's spiritual presence in our lives.

Why Church?
Write a prayer in which you talk to God about your deepest feel-ings and wishes for your friends. Share with the group, if you desire, or keep the prayer personal.

Into the World
Pray together the prayer that is part of the Prayer of Thanks-giving in the Communion Service: "In remem-brance of these your mighty acts in Jesus Christ, we offer ourselves in praise and thanksgiving as a holy and living sacri-fice, in union with Christ's offering for us, as we proclaim the mystery of faith. Christ has died; Christ is risen; Christ will come again. All honor and glory is yours, almighty God, now and forever. Amen."

PUT IT ALL TOGETHER

This session re-examines the link between spiritual growth and God's love.

NO ONE IS WORTHY, NOTHING IS EARNED

Anthony: I'd like to think I've grown stronger over the past few years as I've consciously practiced spirituality. I'm struggling, however, with the feeling that we're not supposed to earn grace. I *know* that we *don't* earn grace. I haven't quite reconciled these two things. God's grace is unearned, yet we're supposed to seek it through worship and spirituality.

Anisa: This is probably a poor analogy, but here goes. I ordered some furniture a few months ago. The store said they'd come on a certain day within a certain four-hour period. So I had to be ready for them. But see, God's more faithful than that! God doesn't conform to our expectations; and if you think about it, we really wouldn't want him to.

Give incoming members a small present (a small bag of M&Ms®, for example). Explain that it is a free gift with no strings attached.

What was the best gift you ever received? Had you done anything to deserve it? Relate your feelings toward the gift of God's grace. When do we respond ungratefully, humbly, happily?

My boyfriend says my expectations change constantly! Maybe God messes with us a little, just to see if we're paying attention. Jesus hung out with prostitutes and extortionists. He picked Paul, a hate-filled person, to be an apostle. He also became available to people who were actively looking for him.

It's all a big mystery, but God's love is in the mystery.

A GOSPEL FOR EVERYONE

Paul was amazed that the gospel was for everyone. He had been used to a religion aimed at his own religious/ethnic group, the Jewish people. Correctly understood, the Old Testament teaches that God loves non-Jews, too. In Christ, however, God extended a close relationship to Jews and non-Jews.

All of us, in turn, can cultivate that close relationship from our side. When he walked the earth, Jesus was usually critical of the religious "experts." Why? Because they used spiritual practices to define who was worthy of God

SMALL GROUP

Friends
Form teams of two or three. What kinds of friends do you have? Do you have friends among ethnic or economic groups other than your own? Do you get together socially with friends? Do you have more acquaintances than friends? Briefly describe your friendships.

and who was not. Christianity is often expressed in that way. Through prayer, worship, and volunteerism, we should get results in our faith. Unfortunately, Christianity sometimes is perceived as a way to become worthy of God's grace. The church becomes an in-group. "We" are going to heaven, and people who have not done all the right things to get into the in-group are going to hell.

Jesus gravitated to those who did not have everything figured out. He did not scold persons about attending worship. He praised people when they had faith, even just a little bit.

FREEDOM IN CHRIST

Paul talks about the freedom of Christ (Galatians 5:1). Christ sets us free because we find our identity in him, not in someone or something else. Christ calls us out of our familiar patterns and self-defeating behaviors in order to establish us as his people. Christ gives us the freedom to love others. The Great Commandment centers this love upon God, others, and self (Luke 10:27). Love presupposes an inner strength.

Spiritual discipline is not a form of exercise. When we seek God through the practice of spiritual disciplines, we do not get "better at religion" the same way we get better at tennis. Rather, spiritual discipline offers a variety of ways through which God works in our lives. Discipline

Freedom in Christ
Imagine people saying these things:
- "I really don't feel good about myself, and I've never had a close friend. But I really like you. You didn't return my call the other day."
- "Hey, good to see you! Great outfit, but blue really isn't your color, is it? A tight fit in those slacks? Let's plan to go to my gym next Friday!"
- "I know you need a friend in your situation, and if you want, I'll listen! I'll call you to see how you're doing. You're looking good!"

What do these quotes say to you about the speakers?

Certain people give us clues that they feel insecure or that they feel superior (which may also be insecurity) when they try to be our friends. Other people have a knack for saying the right things. What connections do you see between growing as a Christian and growing in inner strength?

Fruit Bearing
Look at pictures of a produce market or go to a grocery store and look at the produce section. How is food grown, and where does it come from? What does it take to get food to grow? What analogies do you see between the produce and growing spiritually?

helps make us "fruit bearing" people (John 14:5). Because we no longer live in a predominantly agricultural society, the term *fruit bearing people* seems a bit odd. However, the idea is clear. "Fruit" or produce is something that grows and, in turn, nourishes other people. We grow in the fruit of the Spirit, and through us the Spirit touches other people.

REVIEWING SPIRITUALITY

In Session One we discussed the four spiritual types listed by Corinne Ware in her book *Discover Your Spiritual Type*.

Head Spirituality. These people like to think through religious ideas. They appreciate theological concepts, thought-provoking sermons, study groups, books, and writing (essays, journals). They find God through words.

Who You Are Spiritually
Form a plan not only for growing spiritually according to your preferred type, but also for growing in communion with other people. (Reread "What Is the Evidence?" pages 23-24.) What is God guiding you to do with members? How is God leading you to practice forgiveness, to serve others, and to bring hope to others? What comparisons can you make between individual and personal spiritual growth?

Heart Spirituality. These people find God through emotions and emotional experiences. They are deeply touched by music, by evangelism and testimony, upbeat and spontaneous church services, and internal spirituality.

Mystic Spirituality. People of a more mystical turn also appreciate internal spirituality, and they find spiritual meaning in contemplative, often non-verbal prayer, and in a simple lifestyle. They are happy to sit silently, waiting for God to speak to the inner, intuitive self.

Kingdom Spirituality. These people find God through action. They want to see the world become a better place. They want to work for some idea and to enlist others to strive for the same vision.

WHO YOU ARE IS FINE

All of us have tendencies in more than one of the spirituality categories. Ware writes, "Knowing your chief tendency will help you understand that what and who you are *is just fine.* You do not need to have the same desires as others. The Creator has made you to find your connection to the Holy in a particular way. Our spiritual formation comes from both nature and nurture; temperament and environment" (page 84). She notes that one of her friends was always discontented at his church, but once he understood his spiritual tendencies, he realized that his church was at the opposite spiritual side. He stayed at that church, but he also stopped castigating himself as a bad church member. Now he "feeds" his spirituality in other ways (page 85).

Knowing your chief tendency does not mean that you will concentrate all your spiritual explorations in that particular way.

DISCUSS

Spiritual Types
Consider hosting a workshop for your congregation in order to help people understand spiritual types. Confer with your pastor about ideas.

As an additional option, think about the spiritual type of your congregation. What do you consider your church's strengths? weaknesses? What do you consider its predominant spiritual type to be? What is your own predominant type, and how does it fit with the spiritual type of your church's?

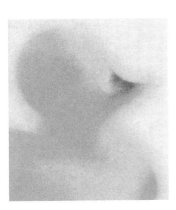
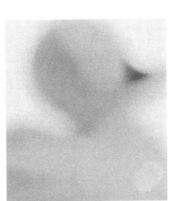
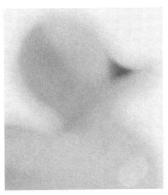

Thomas Merton, a Trappist monk and author, wrote books on theology; but he also enjoyed drawing, doing calligraphy, writing poetry, taking photographs, and being with friends. Just as we appreciate different occupations and hobbies, we grow spiritually in various ways.

BEING FORMED

Growth, whether emotional or spiritual or both, is rarely easy, especially as we become adults and begin to fall into familiar patterns. We often do not know how we need to grow until we are in situations that force us to see ourselves clearly. Those situations are often difficult ones: family or personal crises, serious mistakes, uncertain choices, or illness.

We are always being formed by something: parental expectations, job pressures, career dreams, and goals. We are also formed in subtle ways by social messages. We are supposed to look like those magazine models. We are supposed to dress in certain ways. We are supposed to purchase certain products. Even media reports about health issues take on the quality of social pressure. What are the medical pundits saying this week about what to eat and what to avoid?

When we realize how much pressure there is to conform to someone's expectations, we long for something different. We survey the people we know and the people we see at the mall, the market, and in class. We long for something that grounds us as a unique person.

LOOK CLOSER

Being Formed
During the week, clip articles from newspapers or news magazines that deal with either sports people in training or health and dietary issues. Also clip photographs and advertisements that communicate certain body images and particular foods. Do you think our society pushes people to look or behave or eat in certain ways? Are those messages consistent or contradictory? What guidelines does your religious faith provide in sorting through social expectations?

MARKETING SPIRITUALITY

Books on spirituality have flooded the market. According to *Fortune* magazine (July 9, 2001), Big Business is interested in developing spirituality, although books like *Christianity Incorporated*, by Michael Budde and Robert Brimlow (Brazos Press, 2002) criticize the capitalism-flavored brands of spirituality. That same *Fortune* article notes that 95 percent of Americans, compared to about half of Western Europeans, believe in God; and 78 percent of Americans polled want to grow spiritually. Looking for books about spirituality, you would hardly go wrong concentrating on texts that are true to Jesus' teachings, Old and New Testament Scriptures, and Christian tradition. One of the service learning exercises at the end of this book provides a few possibilities. Pastors can also provide helpful direction.

Books About Spirituality
Log onto *amazon.com* or *barnesand-noble.com*. See how many books they provide if you simply type in the key word *spirituality*. The list will probably be very long, but take some time to notice particular authors, titles, and subjects of interest. Then type in the names of authors like Henri Nouwen, Thomas Merton, Reuben Job, Roberta Bondi, and others you noticed. Start making a "to read" list of spirituality authors whom you would like to study.

JULIE'S NOTES

"Okay, I'm still thinking about that guy in my philosophy class. Even though I think he was being too defensive, I started going through Paul's letters. I tried to see what Paul said about the gospel. Well, 'ask and ye shall receive.' The good news of Jesus is

- forgiveness of our sins through the blood of the cross (Romans 5:8-9)
- God's justification and redemption of us (Romans 3:21-26)
- reconciliation between God and us, through Christ (Romans 5:10-11)

73

- a mortal blow against the powers of evil in the world (1 Corinthians 15:24-28)
- the assurance that we are God's beloved children in Christ (Galatians 4:7)
- Christ's perfect sacrifice, demonstrating God's righteousness (Romans 3:23-26)
- the assurance of God's free gift of mercy and salvation (Romans 6:23)
- God's identification with human suffering and death (Philippians 2:5-8)
- the removal of barriers that separate us (Galatians 3:27-29; Ephesians 2:14-16)
- the defeat of the power of sin and death/the transformation of our mortal, physical bodies into spiritual, eternal bodies (1 Corinthians 15:51-57)
- God's promise never to forsake us and his promise never to allow anything to separate us from his love (Romans 8:31-39).

"I'm still searching spiritually, but I think I understand why Paul gave up everything in order to get close to Christ.

"He destined us for adoption as his children through Jesus Christ, according to the good pleasure of his will. In him we have redemption through his blood, the forgiveness of our trespasses, according to the riches of his grace that he lavished on us. With all wisdom and insight he has made known to us the mystery of his will. In him you also, when you had heard the word of truth, the gospel of your salvation, and had believed in him, were marked with the seal of the promised Holy Spirit. This is the pledge of our inheritance toward redemption as God's own people, to the praise of his glory" (Ephesians 1:6-9, 13-14).

CLOSE

Into the World
Light a candle, and think about various mysteries made known.
- The Holy Spirit
- Jesus' death and resurrection
- God's grace
- Fruit of the Spirit
- Eternal life
- Our adoption as God's children
- Forgiveness of our sins
- God's guidance when we are confused
- God's promise of heaven

What about God still seems strange and mysterious? What about God now seems happy and comforting?

CASE STUDIES

Getting Started

Use any of these cases in place of or in addition to the cases in the sessions as a means of stimulating discussion.

Case 1: Ted

Ted recently had a life-changing experience. He has attended church his entire life but recently felt that something was missing in his life. He is 31 years old, makes good money at his firm, and he is married to Sharon. His two sons, Justin and Ryan, attend preschool. Lately, his boss has been hassling him, but Ted tries to brush off his feelings of resentment. Sharon wants him to contribute more to the upkeep of the house, but Ted is always too tired when he gets home late in the evening after a long commute.

Recently Ted stopped by his church after work and went inside for a few moments. It had been a particularly difficult day. As he prayed, he felt overwhelmed with a feeling of peace. The feeling seemed to come for no particular reason. At the time he was leafing idly through a hymnal. Ted's emotional turmoil vanished as if washed away. He felt cleansed. Ted could not wait to go home and tell his family.

Sharon, who grew up in church and never heard of such a thing, was incredulous. However, Ted felt as if for the first time the whole meaning of what it means to be a Christian came together for him.

- What do you think happened to Ted?
- How was his spiritual experience related to his life situation?
- If you were Sharon, how would you respond?

Case 2: Christa

First Church was a typical sort of congregation in a medium-sized town. The choir director/organist had been on the job for several years. One Sunday, a young adult Sunday school class suggested an upbeat, contemporary song for the worship service. "Could the choir sing this sometime?" asked Christa, a class member.

The director heard the request as "We don't like the songs the choir sings" and responded, in no uncertain terms, that she did not take requests!

Resentment simmered in Christa's class. Two families stopped coming to the class, though they came to worship. Christa discussed the matter with the pastor, who had been quarrelling with the choir director about budget matters. Unfortunately, the pastor had little input about the music dispute, and the problem continued.

Several more people stopped attending First Church before Christa received a call from another class member, Denise. She said, "We're starting a break-off congregation at my house. Are you with us?"

- How would you have helped to solve this problem if you were Christa? the pastor? the choir director?
- How do you think a knowledge of spiritual types could be helpful in the circumstances described?

Case 3: Cassandra

Cassandra had never imagined being in the emergency room with a stroke, especially at 32 years old. Her physician told her that the stroke was a rare side effect of taking birth control pills. Eventually Cassandra got back on track. Her mother came to town to help take care of Cassandra's daughter.

Since her recovery, Cassandra has felt stressed out. Though she has rarely felt frightened, she now has become apprehensive and insecure. Her brush with death has made her think deeply about many things, especially her relationship with God. Until the stroke, she had been a reasonably faithful churchgoer. She wants to raise her daughter in church, but she is not even sure she has a relationship with God. She wants a fresh start, but she does not know where to begin.

- Have you ever experienced a brush with death? How did that experience affect your religious life?
- What might Cassandra do to jump-start her relationship with God? Who might she talk to? Where should she turn first?

Case 4: Deborah

Deborah referred to her husband, Bill, and his family as "Bible-thumping fanatics." They consider her an infidel (an unbeliever) because she wants proof for what she believes. Deborah responds to several of her family's assertions below:

It says so in the Bible, and the Bible is God's Word. "How do you know it's God's Word?" Deborah would respond. "That's not proof. Muslims believe the Qur'an is God's Word. Hindus believe the Bhagavad Gita is God's Word. Mormons believe the Bible plus the Book of Mormon are God's Word. Which one is really God's Word?"

Jesus fulfilled all the prophecies, and that cannot be a matter of chance. "Why not?" Deborah would respond. "The prophecies were public knowledge. Why couldn't Jesus' disciples write about his life so that it looked as if he fulfilled the prophecies?"

Archaeological evidence supports the Bible. "Not necessarily," Deborah would respond. "They find Noah's Ark every few years in Turkey! No one can prove that the tomb near Jerusalem is Jesus', let alone that he rose from the dead. And speaking of evidence, where are the dinosaurs in Genesis? Where did Cain get his wife? In the Book of Joshua, God stopped the sun. How could he do that when it's really the earth's rotation?"

Bill and his family tell Deborah that they are afraid she is going to hell unless she gets her heart right. Deborah wants to find someone who can answer her questions without becoming defensive and judgmental.

- Do you feel more sympathetic for Deborah or for her relatives?
- Besides avoiding the subject of religion entirely, what might help Deborah and her relatives achieve some common ground?
- If Deborah cannot find common ground with her relatives, what might she do to have her questions answered?
- Do you think intellectual curiosity alone accounts for Deborah's questions? Why or why not?

SERVICE LEARNING OPTIONS

Enhance your group's understanding of balanced Christian living by implementing some of the service or learning projects mentioned below.

IDEA 1: Study Spiritual Types

Get a copy of *Discover Your Spiritual Type: A Guide to Individual and Congregational Growth*, by Corinne Ware (The Alban Institute, 1995). The book can be ordered from your local bookstore or over the Internet from *amazon.com* or *barnesandnoble.com*. In Chapters 1 through 3, Ware discusses spiritual types. In Chapter 4, "Using the Spirituality Wheel Selector," she gives a short exercise for discovering one's spiritual strengths and preferences. This exercise is very helpful for matching your spiritual type with your congregation's predominant style. Chapter 5 provides several workshop models for congregations seeking to discover their spiritual styles, and Chapter 6 provides plans for church growth. She notes that congregations need not switch styles entirely; that would be very difficult and very counterproductive. In subsequent chapters she provides ideas for personal spiritual growth. Read Ware's book either for yourself or as part of a study group and discuss insights you gain by working through the ideas presented.

IDEA 2: *Lectio Divina*

Chapter 8 of *Discover Your Spiritual Type* discusses the ancient practice of reading Scripture called *Lectio Divina* (translated as "sacred reading"). There are four different ways of reading the Bible:

Reading: involving the senses. As you read a Bible passage, think about its characters and setting.
Use your imagination to think about the sights, smells, and sounds of the passage.
Meditating: involving reflection and thinking. Think about the meaning and significance of the passage.
Prayer: involving feelings. What are your emotional responses to the passage?
Contemplation: involving intuition. As you relax and stay quiet, clearing your mind, what thoughts or images arise in your heart, your inner sense, spontaneously? If you don't have any such thoughts, return to the Bible passage.

Ware recommends setting aside several minutes for this exercise. How might you find a pattern in your life for this kind of reading on a regular basis? Depending on your "spiritual type" you'll find one or more of these exercises more meaningful, though all can be helpful in understanding the Bible. This exercise can be used for individuals or for small groups.

IDEA 3: Church Shop

When they move to a new area, they "shop around" for a church that they like. Plan a "church shopping" itinerary to discover different kinds of worship styles and emphases. You might check the Yellow Pages first. Many churches have multiple services on Sunday morning, each with "contemporary" or "traditional" services. Many churches also have services on Wednesday evenings and Saturday evenings. For more information about different Christian traditions, check out *Handbook of Denominations in the United States*, by Frank S. Mead, Samuel S. Hill, and Craig D. Atwood (11th Edition, Abingdon Press, 2001).

You may have to overcome your self-consciousness about "popping in" at a church in which you may very well not know what's going on. Be aware that many churches are, intentionally or not, ethnically homogeneous. You may be the only person of your ethnic group in attendance. Also be aware that many churches love to follow up on first-time visitors with personal visits, phone calls, loaves of bread, literature, and so forth. If you don't want to be visited, make your desire clear.

Once you're there, relax and enjoy the worship. What seems to be the most meaningful aspect of worship for the regulars? What is most meaningful to you? If you attend several churches over a period of time, write down your ideas and impressions. Ask: What was the most important aspect of the congregation?

IDEA 4: Spiritual Formation Study

Find an edition of the Bible that aims specially at spiritual formation. *The Spiritual Formation Bible*, for instance, is published by Zondervan and can be purchased in the New Revised Standard Version or the New International Version—two fairly recent translations of the Bible that are very popular in many churches for their accuracy and readability. You can order the book from your bookstore, online, or from Zondervan at 800-232-5010. Another such Bible is the *Serendipity Bible for Groups* in the New International Version, published by Serendipity House (800-525-9563), a well-known resource of study materials for church small groups.